THE LIGHT AFTER DEATH

THE LIGHT AFTER DEATH

My Journey to Heaven and Back

VINCENT TODD TOLMAN

with LYNN TAYLOR

Published by Ascendt Publishing
www.TheLightAfterDeath.com

Book cover design by Wizdiz
Book interior design by Eden Graphics, Inc.

ISBN 978-1-958626-00-9
Library of Congress: pending

Printed and bound in the United States of America

10 9 8 7 6 5 4 3 2 1

In honor of the light and divinity within you, this book is dedicated to you.

Death is nothing more than a doorway,
something you walk through.

— Dr. George G. Ritchie,
author of *Return from Tomorrow*

FOREWORD

By Richard Paul Evans

#1 New York Times bestselling author

During my early twenties I experienced what the poet St. John of the Cross called the "Dark Night of the Soul." I was in spiritual crisis. I had suffered a terrifying emotional breakdown while serving on a church mission and had never felt so confused, alone or betrayed. I was angry with God for abandoning me when I needed Him the most. I began to question many of my long-held beliefs about God and religion. I began to question God's love.

It was during this time that I picked up a book that I found sitting on the receptionist's desk at the advertising agency I worked at—a book called *Return from Tomorrow*. The book was written by Dr. George Ritchie. I would later learn that this little book had sold more than two million copies and was not only one of the first near-death experience (NDE) books, but was, arguably, the most important one ever written. I also learned that this book was the catalyst for the groundbreaking and bestselling book, *Life After Life* by Dr. Raymond Moody.

When I asked our receptionist what the book was about, she told me it was written by a man who was clinically dead for ten minutes and what he had experienced on the "other side of the veil." She said that it was one of the most important books she had ever read.

Given my state of mind at that time, I wasn't looking for a book about God, but I was curious at how profoundly moved she was by the book, so I decided to give it a chance. I had a rare, quiet afternoon, and I took the book up into my office and began to read.

Though I had planned to read only the first chapter, I never put it down, finishing the book that afternoon. The book answered questions I had been struggling with and, more importantly, restored my hope and faith in God. I felt spiritually and emotionally whole again, and I was grateful that Dr. Ritchie had written this important book. At the time, I had no idea that someday Dr. Ritchie and I would become friends.

It was nearly seven years after reading Dr. Ritchie's book that I wrote my first book—a holiday novella called *The Christmas Box*. At its peak, my little book was an international bestseller and, for five weeks, held the number one spot on the *New York Times*, *Wall Street Journal*, and *USA Today* bestsellers list.

It was a surprising accomplishment for a book that, initially, no one wanted to publish. After a myriad of rejections from publishers, I decided to self-publish it. That was back in 1992, long before the existence of on-demand publishing. There were no online book sellers back then, no Amazon or BN.com. For the most part, books were sold through small, mom-and-pop bookstores. That required that I attended a lot of bookseller conventions to introduce my book to booksellers, hoping that they would sell it in their stores.

It was at one of these conventions—the Mountains and Plains booksellers in Colorado—that I saw on the program that Dr. Ritchie was going to be speaking on a panel with several other authors of near-death experience books. At the time, Betty J. Eadie's book, *Embraced by the Light*, was one of the bestselling books in America, and people were fascinated with the topic of near-death experiences.

I learned that I wasn't alone in my fascination. The meeting was packed, and every seat was full. I ended up standing, with many others, at the back of the hall for the entire hour.

There were three authors sharing their experiences. The first author to speak was a woman named Ranelle Wallace, author of *The Fire Within*. What made Ms. Wallace's story especially credible (and sympathetic) was that her cause of death was a plane crash, and she had suffered third degree burns over much of her body—a fact that was clearly observable.

In contrast, the second author was far less credible. In fact, I quickly pegged him as just another gold digger, claiming his share of the NDE mother lode that Mrs. Eadie had unearthed.

After he shared his somewhat bizarre though highly creative experience (he claimed to have ridden to heaven, accompanied by a jazz musician playing the most amazing blues, on a trolley car that left behind it a glimmering silver metallic trail like the one left in a snail's wake) the reporters in the room began questioning him, which turned to them openly mocking him. When he was asked if there was any actual evidence for his death, he acted as if the question had never crossed his mind.

He paused for a moment then said, "Well, I kind of worked myself to death." *Worked himself to death? He was a writer.*

The reporter then asked the author if he had ever experimented with LSD, to which the entire room erupted in laughter.

The final author to speak was Dr. Ritchie. It was clear to me that most of the people in the room, like me, had come to hear him. We weren't disappointed. Dr. Ritchie spoke softly and intelligently, but with such an understated conviction that no one dared challenge what he shared. He spoke with quiet confidence, as simply and frankly as one recounting a recent vacation that could have been anywhere—Paris, New York, or, in his case, death.

I was powerfully moved. Dr. Ritchie was the real deal, a highly esteemed American psychiatrist who held lofty positions as President of the Richmond Academy of General Practice, chairman of the Department of Psychiatry of Towers Hospital, and founder and president of the Universal Youth Corps, Inc.

After the panel concluded, I hurried up to the front of the room to get a closer look at this fascinating man. Dr. Ritchie was being escorted off the stage by his publicist when I shouted out, "Dr. Ritchie."

He turned back to me. "Yes, sir."

"Your book changed my life."

He looked at me for a moment then smiled and said, "For the better, I hope."

Then his publicist grabbed his arm, mumbling frantically that Dr. Ritchie was late for his book signing and didn't have time to talk.

I wanted to get copies of his book to share with my family, so I went out to the convention's book signing room to find him but discovered that he wasn't where he was supposed to be. Disappointed, I was walking away down a crowded hall when someone tapped me on the shoulder. I turned around to see Dr. Ritchie. All he said was, "We need to talk."

After we had found a quiet place away from the crowds, I asked him why he wasn't signing books. He replied with surprising calmness, "Apparently, my books were lost. But it's okay. I feel that God wants me to talk to you."

Why would he feel compelled to talk to me? I wondered.

For the next hour we casually talked about his experience on the other side of death's door. I asked him direct questions about his experience and was both pleased and amazed by his answers. Most of all, there seemed to be a genuine earnestness in his speech. He really wanted me to understand God's love for me. I became a true believer and, I suppose, a fan. It was the beginning of a friendship.

Six months after that show I had one of the best-selling books in the world and found myself, like Dr. Ritchie, on an extensive book tour. (I also got to know Betty Eadie, author of the #1 bestseller *Embraced by the Light*.)

One afternoon, I received a congratulations from Dr. Ritchie. He told me that he would be in my hometown and said his wife wanted to meet me. He asked if I had time to have lunch with them. I did, of course. Dr. Ritchie and his wife, Marguerite, were lovely and humble. Dr. Ritchie had been flown in to speak at a NDE conference, and he invited me to come hear him speak, an offer I took him up on.

Not once did I hear or see anything that made me question the validity of his experience. Whether he actually spoke to

God or not, I can't honestly know for sure, but there is no question in my mind that Dr. Ritchie believed that he had. It reminds me of something author Stephen King once said to a reporter who questioned him about the origin of his stories. "I don't care if you believe what I told you or not," King said, "just as long as you believe that I believe it."

This was the beginning of my fascination with near-death experiences. Since then, I've talked to many others about their near-death experiences. Truth matters and though I approach each storyteller politely, it is with a healthy dose of skepticism, doing my best to match the story with its teller. So it was when I first encountered Mr. Vincent Tolman.

I met Vincent in Phoenix, Arizona, at a writer's conference I was hosting. Initially, I didn't know that the book Vincent wanted to write was about a near-death experience. What I did know was that he was a humble, kind man, and that his wife and daughter obviously adored him. The better I got to know him, the more I liked him. His ready smile and wry sense of humor drew people to him. (Vincent lives in Las Vegas, so when someone at the event started calling him *Vinney Vegas*, the name stuck. Lol.) He told me how strongly he felt about having to share his experience, but that he didn't know how or where to start.

I counseled him to begin his book by speaking out his story, recording everything he could remember of the experience. He did as I advised then sent me the digital file. With my busy schedule and book deadlines, it was a few months before I found time to listen to his audio recording.

Frankly, I was astonished by what I heard. With the exception of Dr. Ritchie's book, I had never heard an NDE experience that profound. Vincent's recountment was not only fascinating, but, more importantly, enlightening. I found myself frequently pondering on what I had learned from his experience and used his insight as a filter to better understand our world and its growing chaos. Through time, I became more and more enlightened and soon felt, like Vincent, that his story needed to be shared.

What you are holding in your hands is the result of that arduous journey. It is my hope that you have an experience like the one that I had in reading this book, one of enlightenment and peace—one that fills you with hope and greater love not only for God, but for all His creations. Simply put, I hope you find in Vincent's journey precisely what you need in your journey. May God bless you to that end.

PREFACE

By Lynn Taylor

THIS BOOK CHANGED MY LIFE. It changed me. I am a different person now than I was when I was first introduced to Vincent's story. Of course, like most internal changes, it was a process. Elevating who you are rarely happens in an instant.

I met Vincent (I've only ever known him as "Vinney") at a dinner event for men seeking to make a positive difference in the world. There were dozens of men there, and the buzz of activity made it difficult to have a deep and meaningful conversation. Vinney and I sat across from each other, and we exchanged what stories we could over the busy dinner.

The evening ended, and we parted ways, perhaps never to meet again. When it was over, I remembered two things about Vinney.

First, that he had had an interesting near-death experience. I still have trouble calling it a "near" death experience, though. To me, being in a body bag is beyond "near." I hadn't learned many details of his experience, such as the deep lessons he learned, but I remembered that he had more than a brief peek through the door to the other side.

The second thing that I remembered about Vinney was his humble sincerity. He was very matter-of-fact about the experience, as if he was talking about a trip he had taken, or a school he had attended. He was one of the most gracious and unassuming people I had ever met, and that impressed me.

I was raised with a belief in "the other side," and that there are forces active in our lives that exist beyond our physical senses. While I knew that we have access to senses beyond our mortal ones, I was never confident that mine were very keen. I had seen those senses in action with other people many times, but my own experience with them had been fleeting and, in some cases, unreliable (or so I thought).

We met again at a writers' retreat hosted by *New York Times* bestselling author Richard Paul Evans at his ranch in southern Utah. I was working on a novel, and Vinney had been striving to translate his experience into a book.

One afternoon after lunch, Vinney and I sat in the front room of the ranch house, stretched out on oversized bean bags, talking about our writing projects. I was surprised when Vinney asked me if I would help him put his experience into words. What surprised me more than his question was that I said "yes," almost without a thought. I wasn't sure that I was the right person for the task, but I trusted Vinney's judgment and also followed my intuition. It just felt like the right answer, and I was confident that it would somehow all work out.

Vinney sent me a transcript of an audio recording he made, recounting his death and what he learned on the other side. It was my first encounter with the full scope of his journey, and it fascinated me. It was remarkable to me how closely the lessons he learned aligned with my life experience thus far. I'm not referring to the details of existence after we die—I mean the principles of how to have a more fulfilling and rewarding life while we are still here. Insights that he shared brought my lifetime of hazy inferences and fuzzy assumptions into clear and focused principles, and that excited me.

As I worked on the book, I also started to recognize thoughts and ideas that were not my own. In the weeks and months that followed, as I wrote and rewrote, I often had questions that I would need to ask Vinney about. Then I noticed that I sometimes received answers almost as soon as I thought of the question. The answers would enter my thoughts gently, like a whisper that I had to be ready to hear. I would always verify the details with Vinney, but time after time, all Vinney did was confirm the answer I had already been given, and perhaps add some additional details.

What is most remarkable to me is that I can now look back at a lifetime of receiving similar whispers and, in those moments of guidance and inspiration, not recognizing them for what they were. My self-doubt had dimmed my inner senses to the spectacular unseen realities of existence surrounding me.

My wife, Donna, has always had a strong sensitivity to spiritual things. Some time after the first draft was complete, she said, "Whenever I walked by your office, I could always tell when you were working on Vinney's book."

"How could you tell?" I asked.

"It just felt different. Like there were other people there."

She was right. They were involved from the very beginning. It just took me time, and no small amount of practice and effort, to develop my spiritual senses enough to recognize their input. I am deeply grateful for their help, not only because of the help itself, but because of the skills I have gained as a result. I can't say that I am perfect at listening to the advice and guidance I receive, but I am better at it now. I can now confidently add my voice to the growing chorus that sings that we are not alone in this life. We never truly are.

There is another gift that this book brought into my life. The principles in this book have changed the way I see our world, the universe, and my place in it. Life may be challenging, but the way to have a rich and fulfilling life is really quite simple. The principles in this book provide a universally applicable guide on how to start.

I am different now than when I started on this path, and I am deeply grateful for the many gifts that made that transformation happen. I still can't see more than a few steps ahead of where my winding path will take me, but I carry a quiet, firm assurance of where that path ultimately leads. I am also better prepared to make the most of this journey, wherever the road may roam.

My hope is that your experience with this book will do the same for you.

AUTHOR'S NOTE

I died on Saturday, January 18, 2003. This fact is not in dispute. I was cut out of a body bag. I still have a piece of it. When the EMTs found me in the bathroom of a Dairy Queen, my body temperature was 79 degrees, and I had been dead for 45 minutes. Maybe longer.

This book is my attempt to tell you about the events leading up to my death, what I learned while on the other side of death, and my experiences after I was brought back to life. I say *attempt*, because though I have done my best to explain what happened, the nature of existence on the other side is so different from this world, that explaining it poses a unique challenge—like explaining a sunset to someone who has never seen one, or the flavor of salt to someone who has never tasted it. I remember what I saw, I just don't always know how to accurately describe it. The best I can do is relate it to things that we know here on Earth.

First of all, I refer to God as "He" throughout this book. As a Christian, I identify God as being male and the Creator of the universe. Whatever your faith or tradition, use your own name or vision for God. I learned in my progress that the Creator has many names across many cultures, religions, and belief systems. Our Creator created each of us, loves us, and answers to all of the names and concepts that we use when we reach out to Him.

While I was separated from my body, I went on a journey through another level of existence. I was accompanied by a guide who taught me ten fundamental principles to help me progress toward a glorious destination. When we live in harmony with these principles, we elevate our being and draw closer to our Creator. These foundational principles are:

Be authentic

Understand the purpose of life

Love everyone

Listen to your inner voice

Use technology responsibly

Release prejudice

Exercise the power of creation

Avoid negative influences

Understand the purpose of evil

Know that we are all one

Communication and learning on the other side of Death did not happen exactly as I describe. In this book, my learning is presented as a conversation, because that is how we communicate on Earth. When my guide shared information with me in the Spirit Realm, it happened more like a data download to my mind, and I would unpack and process the information as we travelled toward our destination.

Learning a principle is like smelling spaghetti sauce. You instantly recognize that it's spaghetti sauce, but if you pay attention, you can begin to pick out the ingredients: the garlic, oregano, and other herbs. The concept of a principle was like smelling the sauce, and the deeper understanding of the implications and applications of a principle came to my awareness when I analyzed it more deeply.

It is my sincere hope that my experience will help you in your own life journey, and help you recognize and connect with the love of God more fully in your life. He is real, and He knows and loves you—specifically and uniquely YOU—more than you realize.

PART I

Chapter 1

THE DAY I DIED

THE ONLY THING ON MY MIND when I woke up on that cold January morning was that I had the entire day off from my construction job. It was a Saturday, and I was going to make the most of it. I didn't think to call my mom to tell her that I loved her. I didn't think about all of the things I had left undone, the friends I would leave behind, and the family who would miss me. I didn't know I would die that day.

I rolled out of bed and hopped in the shower, envisioning my day. I planned to meet up with my best friend Rob, grab a quick bite to eat, work out at the gym, then go downtown to the annual International Auto Expo in Salt Lake City.

I rushed through my morning routine, grabbed my car keys, threw on my winter jacket, and stepped out into the cold. The pearl white of my Mitsubishi Eclipse looked almost gray under the blanket of clouds that couldn't decide whether or not to snow. I slid into the driver's seat, fired up the engine, and backed out of the driveway.

The drive to my buddy's house was short enough that the car heater didn't even have time to warm up the cold interior, but it gave me time to reflect on how much Rob had changed my life in just a few short months. Rob had ignited a passion for health and fitness in me. We had literally spent hundreds of hours together between working a health-related business, working out, and getting stronger. We shared our research and discoveries with each other, including new nutrition supplements that would help us be even stronger and healthier. Life was great, and full of promise.

Rob lived in a quiet neighborhood in Orem, just a few miles from my house. I parked in front of Rob's house and ran up to the door, giving a quick courtesy knock as I let myself in.

"Hey, Rob. You ready?"

Rob's voice carried up from downstairs, "I'll be right up."

I noticed a plain brown box, about the size of a large drink bottle, on the kitchen table. The white shipping label gave me a clue to its contents.

"Is this that new supplement you ordered a few weeks ago?" I yelled down to him.

"Yeah, bro," Rob said as he bounded up the stairs. "I'm excited to try it." His dark hair was still damp. He was strong and lean, a little shorter than me. His infectious smile lit up his gray-green eyes. "Let's take some before we hit the gym."

Rob tore open the package and lifted out a large white plastic bottle. Its colorful label was printed in a foreign, Asian-looking script.

"Where is this from?" I asked.

"I ordered it from Thailand," he said. "All of the U.S. suppliers were sold out. It should be the same as the American stuff, though."

Rob carefully poured the clear liquid into the bottle's cap and drank it. He measured another and handed it to me. I downed it in a gulp. The supplement we normally took tasted like lemon water. This one tasted sour and bitter.

Almost as soon as the drink passed my lips, I knew something was wrong. Within seconds, a coldness crept from my belly through my body. I turned to Rob. "Did that taste weird?"

He looked concerned. "Something's different with this stuff. I don't feel so good."

"Me either. Let's get something to eat. That might help."

"Good idea. I'll drive."

We walked out to Rob's Nissan Maxima. He backed out of the driveway, and we drove off down the road.

The supplement's peculiar effect intensified. Something was very wrong. My thighs felt cold, like they weren't getting enough blood flow. We had only driven a few blocks when Rob's head started to bob, and his eyes fluttered, as if he was falling asleep.

"Rob!" I grabbed his arm and shook him. "Let's stop at the Dairy Queen."

Rob nodded and a moment later pulled into the restaurant's parking lot.

The cold sensation wormed up my spine. Nausea turned my stomach, and I had a sudden, powerful urge to use the bathroom. I was suddenly afraid I was going to make a mess in Rob's car. As soon as he put the car in park, I jumped out.

"I'm going to hit the bathroom," I said. I stumbled through the entrance, down the short hallway, and into the one-seater men's room. I locked the door then, as I walked toward the toilet, the blue tiled walls began to spin. I fell to the floor and passed out.

———

I later learned that Rob was having a similar experience: he slid into a booth, then collapsed on the table, and threw up.

The young shift manager heard Rob's retching and peeked around the corner to investigate. He found Rob lying unconscious in his own vomit, his body shuddering. He dashed back behind the counter and called 911 for an ambulance.

Unfortunately for me, I had fallen on my back and, when I threw up, everything that came out of my stomach was sucked into my lungs, blocking my airway.

That's when I died.

Chapter 2

BEING DEAD

As soon as my head hit the ground, I felt my being completely immersed in a sense of wonderful coolness—like water. I felt weightless, like I was floating in the air. I had the sensation that I was sitting up, and looked around me, trying to see something— anything—but it was as if everything was hidden in a fog.

When the fog gradually cleared, I was looking down at a drama unfolding below me in the dining area of the Dairy Queen. It was like I was watching a movie from a comfortable chair, and the director had decided to shoot every scene from above. But I was also certain that what I was watching was happening in real life.

My attention was so focused on what was happening below me that the strangeness of my situation never crossed my mind, much as when you are in a dream and accept everything that occurs, no matter how surreal.

I saw Rob sprawled over the table of a booth, his vomit covering the table, the seats, and the floor. The restaurant's workers were frantic. I could feel their emotions: worry, fear, concern, helplessness. I could especially feel the angst of the teenage manager. He was tall and skinny with short brown hair, the edges of his bangs frosted with highlights. His baby-blue eyes kept looking up, as if asking for God's help. He kept thinking, "This guy is going to die, and on my watch." And I could hear a woman's voice running through his mind, "If you don't get out of this job, you're going nowhere." I somehow knew that the voice belonged to his mother.

I could feel the workers' relief when a paramedic team rushed through the door. It was suddenly no longer their concern, though I was aware that they were still worried about the poor young man lying unconscious on the table.

The medics loaded Rob onto a gurney then rushed him out to the waiting ambulance and sped away, sirens blaring.

I was worried about Rob and tried to follow, but I couldn't. Every time I tried to move, no matter what direction, some invisible cord prevented me from going beyond the Dairy Queen.

Then I noticed the motionless body of a young man lying on the bathroom floor. He was covered in vomit, too. I knew immediately that he was dead. The body's neck was swollen nearly to the width of the head, and his skin was mottled deep purple, with yellow blotches on the cheeks. The body I was looking at was so grotesque that it appeared fake, like a cheap prop in a B-grade horror movie. I felt pity for the man. I had no idea who he was.

I turned my attention back to the dining area of the restaurant and saw a girl, maybe sixteen or seventeen, wiping up the vomit on the table. Her strawberry blonde hair was tied in a bun, and a black apron covered the front of her blue uniform shirt and black pants. The manager walked over to her, carrying a bucket and mop. I felt their emotions start to calm down as they immersed themselves in the routine of the work.

While they cleaned the booth, a middle-aged couple entered. I could tell they were married. They hesitated when they saw the cleanup in progress but stepped up to the counter and ordered. When their food was ready, they sat down in a booth near the bathroom. I listened to them talking about their son's new wife while they ate.

After a while, the husband stood and walked over to the bathroom. When he found it was locked, he returned to his seat and resumed the conversation. About five minutes later, he tried again. His need to use the bathroom was growing, and this time when he returned to his seat, he remained focused on the door. He waited for another fifteen minutes before he grew impatient and pounded on the door with his fist. He listened for a response and heard a phone ringing in the bathroom. He walked over to the cashier.

"I think someone might be in trouble in the bathroom. The door is locked, and I can hear a phone ringing, but no one is answering."

"I'll let the manager know," the cashier said.

I looked down from above as the manager grabbed the keys from the hook on the wall and walked from the kitchen to the bathroom door. He knocked. No response.

He knocked again, then unlocked the door.

The door swung inward to reveal the body. He knew he was looking at a dead man.

"Oh, my God," the manager gasped. "We have another one. Amanda, call 911!"

The girl grabbed the cordless handset from its cradle on the wall and punched in the numbers. "We have an emergency. We need another ambulance right away." She rattled off the address as she walked to where the manager stood outside the bathroom and handed him the phone.

"Hello? Yes, I'm the manager. Uh huh. Okay." He turned to the girl. "They're saying to check for a pulse on his wrist."

She just stared at him.

"Go on," he said. "Just feel his wrist for a pulse."

Horrified, she dutifully crept into the bathroom. She crouched down next to the body but did nothing.

"Go on," the manager urged her on. "Just feel his wrist."

She pinched the man's wrist between her thumb and forefingers, lifting it a few inches then dropping it immediately.

"He's cold."

"He's cold to the touch," the manager repeated into the phone. He listened for further instructions, then hung up. He said to the girl, "They said to not touch anything. Just step away and secure the room. They're sending an ambulance and the police."

Guests peered around the corner to see what the fuss was about, and the restaurant staff took turns walking back to the bathroom to view the grisly scene. I could feel the sadness emanating from each person as they looked down at the man on the bathroom floor. Only the cook refused to go see. I knew that he had seen death before. He didn't need to see it again.

Ten more minutes passed before another ambulance arrived with flashing lights and a blaring siren. Three paramedics rushed into the room, each carrying a bag of medical gear. One man pulled out a mask with a squeeze bottle while the senior medic in charge sent the third medic back out to the ambulance to get something.

"He's cold already," the head medic said. He opened the body's mouth. "He aspirated vomit." His emotional intensity dropped. "Help me check for wounds."

The two medics worked together to roll the body over and check for signs of injury.

"No sign of foul play," the head medic said.

"He's already starting to get stiff," the other medic replied.

"Yeah. He's probably been dead for thirty to forty-five minutes already."

As they rolled the body back, I could see what they meant. The body wasn't completely rigid, but it was definitely stiff at the joints.

"I'm going to call time of death," the head medic said. I could feel sadness wash through him. "I'll radio it in."

The third medic came back into the room carrying a small case in his hands. The head medic shook his head and said, "He's gone." He pulled out his handheld radio and reported the situation to the dispatcher.

I could tell that the third medic was a rookie, and that this was his first professional experience with death. He was crestfallen.

They had to wait for ten minutes before they received the all clear to bag the body. They put the body in a bright yellow body bag, zipped the bag closed, secured the body to a board, then carried it outside to a gurney just outside the ambulance. They strapped the body to the gurney by the ankles, waist, and neck, then hefted the gurney headfirst into the ambulance.

The head medic went back inside, asked the employees about what had happened before they arrived, and guided the restaurant manager through the requisite forms. They shook hands, then the medical team prepared to leave.

Just then a police car pulled into the parking lot. The officer got out and walked over to the medic.

"I told dispatch that you didn't need to come out," the medic said.

"I know," the officer replied. "I was in the area and thought I'd stop by anyway."

The head medic pointed to the ambulance with his thumb. "We've already got the body loaded." He pulled a form from his clipboard and handed it to the officer. "Here's the witness report for you. We're going to recommend a tox screen."

"Sounds good. Thanks."

"Anything else you need from us?"

"No, thanks. Sad thing."

"Yeah. Well, we'll be on our way." The medics closed the ambulance's back doors, secured the storage compartments, and took their seats in the ambulance. It was well past noon when the ambulance slowly pulled away and headed to the county morgue.

Chapter 3

A ROOKIE MOVE

THE MEDICS WERE SOMBER and silent as they drove to the medical examiner's office. I could hear the wandering thoughts of the rookie medic as he sat alone with the body in the back of the ambulance. He tried to figure out what had happened, and what they could have done differently. *I can't believe we lost this one*, he thought. *We didn't even get a chance to really help him. I wish we could have tried.*

I felt his heart ache. I noticed a warm golden light started to blossom around his heart. It looked like a miniature sun was growing inside of him.

Then I heard and felt a rumbling, like an earthquake. I looked at the medics, but they weren't affected; only I could feel it. The rumbling quickly grew more intense, and louder and louder. I became aware that it was happening behind me, and it was approaching fast. As it built to a crescendo, something like a shooting star flashed by my right side and hit the young rookie in his heart.

His whole being lit up. It was like the little sun inside of him went supernova. I heard a powerful and commanding voice from the light declare, "*This one is not dead.*"

The rookie looked around for the source of the voice. I was surprised that he did not act on it right away. The voice was so strong and resonated with such authority and power, it sounded to me like the voice of God, or perhaps someone near to God. Yet, I felt the rookie's doubt and heard his thought: *You just imagined it.*

Unrelenting, the glow brightened and spread from his heart to the crown of his head. As I watched the rookie transform, the voice from the light hit him louder and even more powerfully.

"*This man is not dead!*"

The rookie leaped into action.

It was clear to me that the other two medics in the front of the ambulance had not heard a thing. Even though the other two had far more experience, the light had only connected with and spoken to the rookie.

The rookie moved to the motionless body and quietly unbuckled the straps around the neck and waist, then unzipped the bright yellow body bag all the way down to the knees. *I hope this guy is alive,* he thought. *I hope he has a heartbeat.* He pressed his fingers against the discolored neck, searching for a pulse.

Finding nothing, he moved his hand to the corpse's right arm and tried again. Again nothing. He then tried the inside of the man's right thigh. Still nothing.

He pressed harder until he felt hard tissue. Suddenly, I felt a jolt like static electricity. I knew that he must have felt it, too, because his thoughts shifted from faint hope to frantic action.

He grabbed a tracheotomy kit, made an incision in the young man's throat, and inserted a tracheotomy tube. After the tube was seated, he cut open the man's clothes, attaching defibrillator sticky pads to the body.

His mind raced through his training as he repeated a silent prayer, "Please, God, help me do what I need to do. Please, God, help me."

He turned on the machine, and it sounded a ready tone. Hearing it, the medics in the front seat turned around, horrified.

"What are you doing?" the medic in the passenger seat yelled. "Stop! You're going to get fired."

The rookie ignored him. He knew that the voice he had heard was real. He triggered the defibrillator to shock the body. My vision was filled with a flash of white.

No heartbeat.

The head medic turned around and snapped, "Stop messing around. He's dead. Leave him alone. You need to know when to let go."

The defibrillator signaled that it was charged and ready again. He shocked the body a second time. I didn't see a flash this time. The heart monitor registered a single heartbeat, then nothing.

"This will go in your record," the second medic said. "You'd better stop, or you're going to get fired."

The defibrillator was ready again. The rookie triggered the machine a third time, sending a jolt through the body.

Nothing. And then…a heartbeat. Moderate at first, then stronger and steady.

"I have a heartbeat!"

The medics in the front looked at each other with wide eyes. Then the medic on the passenger side climbed over his seat to aid the rookie.

The ambulance was only minutes away from a fully equipped emergency center. The driver grabbed the radio and rattled off a series of codes to Timpanogos Regional Hospital. He flipped on his lights and sirens and changed course for the hospital.

The two medics worked frantically to prepare the revived body for the hospital. Their hands moved so fast that I could barely follow what they were doing: removing straps, cutting away the rest of the body bag, an injection into the chest, another into the arm. I felt the joy radiating from them, and I shared in their happiness in saving that poor man, whoever he was.

The ambulance pulled into the emergency room entrance where a doctor and two nurses waited with a gurney. The medics rolled their patient out of the back of the ambulance and lifted the board the young man was resting on from one gurney to the other. They slid the board out from under him, then pulled away the tattered remnants of the body bag that still adhered to the man's body.

Joined by another doctor and nurse, the medical team wheeled the body inside and down the hallway. Suddenly, the man started to convulse. A nurse ran to grab straps to secure his flailing limbs. She returned and strapped down his legs, then right arm, and started to strap down the left arm. As she did so, I felt a pull on my own left arm. I reflexively pulled hard against it. At the same time, the man's left arm pulled the strap free from the bed. It was only then that I realized that I was watching my own resuscitation.

The feeling of coolness around me turned bitter cold as fear gripped me. I did not know what was going to happen next. If I had died, then why was I still here? I felt the panic and fear of the medical team doing their best to keep my body alive. Their fear fed my fear, and a dark gray fog closed in around me as I spiraled into a dark despair.

Chapter 4

MY GUIDE

MY PANIC GREW, and I felt helpless to stop it. In an instant, my mind flashed through all of the bad things that I had done in my life. There were so many. In that moment I judged myself, and my ruling was that I wasn't worth saving.

But then I immediately saw all of the good that I had done in my life. I saw these things not only from my own perspective, but also from the perspective of everyone I had helped. Many times, I didn't even know that I was doing good. My influence far exceeded my awareness. I gained a perspective of my whole life in a millisecond.

At that moment, I felt a warmth and brightness behind me, like the sun on a bright summer day. It rested on my shoulders and back, and slowly spread over me. The warmth felt like pure love that suffused my whole being and washed the cold fear away. My worry evaporated as the warmth cleansed me from the angst, pain, and concern about everything I had just witnessed. I turned to face the warmth and light that was filling me. As I turned toward the source of the light, I saw a man.

Standing before me was a man who appeared both middle-aged and timeless. His full head of white hair was shoulder length and stood out around his head, majestic like a lion's mane. His beard, also bright white, ended at the bottom of his chest. He wore what appeared to be a pure white robe that extended to his ankles with loose-fitting sleeves down to his wrists. The robe was open in the front, revealing a white shirt and trousers, and a sash around his waist. A simple golden-cream stole was draped around his neck and over his shoulders, flowing down to the bottom of his robe.

His skin appeared pink, yet glistened, like sand on a sunny beach. What captured my attention, though, were his brilliant blue eyes. They seemed to pierce through me, and I sensed that he somehow knew me.

He looked at me with a loving smile, and I felt an overwhelming sense of tenderness and love radiate from him. I could feel his kindness literally flood my being, and my heart basked in its radiant warmth. My first thought was, "Are you God?"

The man laughed a little. "No, son. I'm not God."

"Are you Jesus Christ?"

He laughed again. "No, son. I'm not Jesus Christ."

"Then who are you?"

"You can call me Drake. I am your guide, and I will escort you in whichever direction you want to go." He gestured back behind me. "You can go back to your body if you wish. Or, if you want to come with me, I will show you how to continue on to the next step in your eternal existence."

I didn't hesitate. I didn't want to go back to that pain and worry and fear. Anything would be better than the bitter cold of those emotions. "I want to go with you, wherever that is."

As we spoke, we slowly glided closer together, as if floating through the air. Drake moved to my side.

"All we have to do is learn together. We'll go to an amazing place where you can heal from your life and prepare for your next role."

My next thought was, I must admit, driven by ego. "What do I have to learn? I'm Christian. I already know everything I need to know to get to heaven."

Drake seemed aware of my thoughts and was amused by my confidence. "Let me show you a little glimpse of what you still have to learn."

He opened my mind to the immensity of just my portion of the universe, and how complex and universal the principles were that he would teach me. In that moment, I was overcome by the immensity of it all. It was a massive information download, bigger than I could absorb, but I saw and understood that there were more forms of life than I could possibly imagine. I understood that these principles went beyond my simple tiny existence and applied throughout all of God's creations everywhere. It was as if someone had said, "I'm going to teach you how to design and build a cruise ship," and in response I lifted up a tiny toy boat and declared, "I already know how, see?"

I was humbled and awed. I felt like a child who had only known my little village my whole life, and who now gazed down on the entire globe.

Through all of our communication, there was no condescension, just kindness. His demeanor helped me feel good about what he taught me, and at the same time made me realize how infantile I had been. There was so much knowledge. I had not even begun to learn even a fraction of it all.

"Okay," I said. "Let's go."

Drake smiled and guided me forward. We glided away from the battle to keep me alive that the doctors and nurses were fighting below me.

"There are many principles and truths that you will need to embrace to be able to go where you want to. I'm going to lead you one step, one principle, at a time to get you there."

As I settled into the journey, I realized that we weren't actually speaking to each other like one person speaks to another on Earth; we communicated mind to mind, spirit to spirit. We each sent and received on a specific frequency, like radio waves, that operated on a much higher level than we verbally communicate as mortals. I was no longer limited by the physical aspects of receiving and understanding information. I would ask a question in my mind, and he would return the answer instantly; I would just hear it in my mind, from him, in his voice. It felt like pure love moving back and forth between us.

We accelerated through space, moving at what seemed like an impossible speed. It felt like we were surrounded by a bubble of white light, but I could see everywhere around us. I had the sense of vast distances, and entire galaxies whizzing past as streaks of light. It was like traveling in an airplane, where you know you are moving at hundreds of miles an hour, but you feel like you are sitting as comfortably as in a chair at home. I looked around me in wonder.

"Would you like to stop and take a look?" Drake asked.

I somehow sensed that my time was limited, and that a detour would mean less learning on the way to our destination. "No, let's keep going."

Drake nodded and slid around in front of me. He faced me and looked into my soul with those eyes.

"I'm going to teach you principles that are essential to your personal growth. It is your choice whether or not to accept them."

"What happens if I don't accept them?"

"Then you go a different way. You can continue in your existence as you are, but that is all. If you want to grow, to increase your capability and fulfill your potential, it all depends on accepting and living by fundamental principles."

"There's no punishment for not accepting them?"

"Only in the sense that you are depriving yourself of greater fulfillment, of greater joy and happiness. So, really, you'd just be punishing yourself."

"I understand."

PART II

Chapter 5

Be Authentic

"The first principle you need to learn is to be authentic," Drake said.

This surprised me. "Really?"

"You were expecting something else?"

"I don't know. I thought maybe love, or obedience, or something like that."

Drake laughed. "Trust me, we'll get there. But the first and most important principle is authenticity. It's vitally important to our soul's purpose and happiness. You see, in the physical realm, we are spiritual beings living in a physical body at a very low…" He hesitated for a moment, then said, "Let's relate this to something you can understand. Let's call it frequency. So, the physical realm operates on a very low frequency. Spirit operates on a very high frequency. In the physical realm, we are both spirit and physical, so we have the capability of being very high-frequency beings or very low-frequency beings. It's a matter of what we attune ourselves to. Does that make sense?"

"Yeah, I think so."

Drake just looked at me.

"I mean, yes. I understand." As I accepted the lesson he taught me, I became aware of my own frequency. I was still very much a novice, but I discovered that I had control over it. Much like breathing, I existed in my natural "neutral" state without even thinking about it, but I could also exercise my will to elevate or lower my frequency.

He smiled and nodded. "Being authentic is bringing the physical and spiritual aspects of yourself together, accepting them as they are, and not being ashamed for the world to know the real you. Don't worry about putting on one face for one side of your life and a different face for a different side of your life."

"You mean like when someone puts on one face to go to church, but then they become a different person when they leave the building?"

"Exactly. But it also applies in other settings. People do the same thing at work, with their friends, even with their own family. They hide their true nature from some group or other. Being authentic is being the same person when you're at work and when you're at home. It's weaving the physical and spiritual parts together, so that all aspects of your personality can be one being. It means being proud of and honest about your strengths, but also acknowledging your weaknesses."

"Why is that so important?"

"Because, until you can find true authenticity in your life, you cannot progress and find true happiness."

"So, it doesn't matter what your weaknesses are? Just embrace them?"

"There's a bit more to it than that. You still want to turn your weaknesses into strengths, but to do that, you have to acknowledge them to begin with. We'll get into all of that. For now, you must accept that you need to be authentic. Authenticity leads to happiness."

"Okay. I can accept that. What's next?"

"There's more to this that you need to understand. When you are not authentic, you seek to hide part of who you truly are. Unlike Earth, you cannot lie in this realm. When you look at someone, you know them instantly and completely, to the core of their being."

I had already experienced that when I saw Drake. I could feel the tenderness and love that defined who he was.

"If you are not comfortable with who you really are," Drake continued, "if you are not honest about that, you will hide away to avoid that scrutiny. Some choose to stay on Earth, clinging to old habits and old lies, because they're not ready or willing to face the truth. They are unwilling to work through their limitations because they refuse to face and acknowledge them. They are ashamed, and so they do not progress."

"It sounds like they don't love themselves."

"Exactly. You see it: the core of authenticity is love. When you truly love yourself, even with your imperfections, then you can truly open yourself up to real growth and progress. Love is like a tangible energy field. It's like electricity, but stronger. It is what powers everything God has made."

"That sounds… powerful." I didn't know what else to say.

I was very aware of how much I had to learn.

"It is a power that we can generate, channel, and use to direct things. It is a true caring about what is going on around you. Once you experience the pure love of God, you will wake in the morning loving the oxygen that you breathe in. It means authentically loving everything, and everyone."

Everyone. I thought about the implications and noticed that I felt a resistance. A slowing down. Like I had been moving through space, but was now moving through water, or against a strong pressure. Something was slowing my progress. I could not move forward. I looked to Drake. "What's happening?"

He looked at me with concern in his eyes. "You're holding onto something. It's keeping you from something greater."

"What is it?"

"Look inside yourself. What do you see?"

I looked and recognized that I had reservations about authentically loving all mankind. I thought of people who had hurt me, some legitimately, some only in my imagination. There were people that I withheld my love from.

I was ashamed, but Drake's tender smile gave me hope. He was aware of my every thought. I saw that he had known this about me from the moment we first met. Perhaps even before. And yet, he loved me anyway.

Drake was showing me how to love everyone despite their weaknesses, despite their failings. He accepted me for who I was, and at the same time, he knew that I could be more.

I followed his example and set my intention to love everyone, including myself, flaws and all. We immediately resumed moving forward at our previous speed. I had no idea how fast we were moving, I thought we had to be traveling faster than the speed of light. I was wondering where we were going when Drake asked me a question.

Chapter 6

THE PURPOSE OF LIFE

"WHY ARE YOU HERE?" Drake asked.

I instinctively knew that he wasn't talking about the two of us right then and there. He meant something larger. He was asking the question that has been explored and debated for thousands of years. Four simple words that ask the deepest of questions.

"I…I don't know." I felt myself slowing down again. I searched for a better answer to Drake's question. "I mean, growing up, I was taught Christian values and principles I should live by—that life was a test to see what kind of soul we have."

Drake smiled, and all of those thoughts were immediately washed away. I was dismayed to discover that I was so very wrong.

"Your mortal existence is not a test. It's more of a classroom, where souls are able to learn, grow, and be sorted."

"What's the difference?"

"With a test, you can pass or fail. But God loves every single spirit and creation—*every single one*. He did not create a system of passing and failing. He created a system where everyone succeeds, but only at the speed that they are able to grow."

"So, it doesn't matter if we follow the rules or commandments?"

"Oh, it definitely matters. It matters a great deal. But not because it's a test that you can fail. It's about how quickly you can progress. When we die, we move on to a specific life that is ready for that progress. Some people can grow really fast, and learn really fast, move on really fast. There are others who cannot progress as fast. They are stuck in addictions and vices. Those addictions and vices prevent us from growing."

I could see what he meant. Just like falling prey to vices can keep us from progressing in this life, they could keep us from progressing in the next life as well.

"So, we can continue to progress after we die?"

"We do indeed."

"And the better we do on earth, the easier it is afterwards?"

"I would say faster rather than easier. Though the higher your frequency, the easier it feels. When you enter this stage of existence, if you are at a lower frequency, you will progress more slowly."

Being my best self still mattered, but in a completely different way than I thought. If life is not a pass or fail test, but rather a way to decide how fast I want to progress, it changes everything—all of the judgment, all of the fear, all of the negative feelings about what this life is, and how I'm falling short—

I can throw all of those bad feelings away and, instead, decide what kind of person I want to be. I can decide how quickly I want to progress. And I will progress as fast as I am ready for.

"So, this progress we make. What does that mean?" I asked Drake. "What is the end goal? What is progress after we die?"

"Remember that the life you have on earth is a reflection of the life you can have afterwards. God has given you this life, and it's up to you to show what you will do with it. After we show what we will do with what He gives us, He wants to give us more love, more responsibilities, and more opportunities to create and grow and love in ways you have never imagined. But you have to be ready for it."

"And that's why we're here? To see how fast we're able to progress after this life?"

"To learn and to practice. You can learn and grow a lot during your mortal existence. It's important to make the most of it. Whatever progress you can make while alive will help you that much more after you move on. Speaking of moving on, let's go a bit farther down the road." Drake stepped back in front of me and looked me in the eyes again.

This new perspective was encouraging. It filled me with hope to know that it was okay that I didn't know all of the answers right now. I was excited to learn everything that Drake had to teach me.

We once again resumed our incredible speed. I became aware of an immense sphere of light in the far distance, growing closer. I focused my attention back on Drake.

Chapter 7

LOVE EVERYONE

"SO, WHAT IS THE NEXT PRINCIPLE?" I asked.

"Let's discuss the role of love in our existence."

"Love? Seems simple enough."

"It is both simpler, and more profound, than you have imagined. Love is the foundation of the universe. The world, the cosmos, the galaxy—all of the universes were created out of true, unequivocal, unconditional, pure love. God loves every single one of his creations. And he has creations all over the cosmos."

"Are there other places like Earth?"

"Actually, those of us on Earth can often be the slow learners."

"What does that mean?"

"Well, for one thing, there are other creations that are much, much further ahead of Earth. Granted, they've had longer to progress than we have, but we humans also tend to make decisions that slow us down."

"Decisions that move us in a different direction than God?"

"Exactly. Free will comes with risks. And we tend to do everything we can to both test our free will, and sometimes even to prove we have it. We like to show that we can make whatever decisions we want to, without regard to the long-term impact."

"The other creations don't have free will?"

"They do, they just tend to be more obedient than we are, and so they progress faster. It's a good thing, too."

"It's good that there are creations better than we are?"

"I didn't say *better*. Remember that God loves all of us equally. And I mean *all* of us. Every single one of his creations. It isn't a competition."

"But you said that it's a good thing. Why is that?"

"Because we need help. A lot of help. These other creations assist us in our current situation. The ones who help us the most, though, are usually either what you would call angels, or they could be loved ones who have passed on and have a connection with you. They help us to accelerate raising our frequency. They are called by God to help us. They help facilitate our growth, and help enhance true, unconditional love in the physical world."

"How do they do that?"

"At its most basic, they pour energy into creating positive effects. They may give promptings that guide you in ways that prevent or mitigate harm, provide strength, or divert the course of an event here or there. Sometimes they help to close doors to help guide you to a better one that is opening.

"Everything they do is out of a sense of selfless service. Their service to you helps them to grow as well, but they are really there to serve your needs. And it is all done out of love."

"Love?"

"Yes. God has created everything—absolutely everything—out of love."

"But I don't always feel love."

"Any time you feel the presence of God, every time you feel love, that is His influence. His *true* influence. The only time you will ever feel anything other than love is because of the influence of mortality."

I sensed a hesitation from Drake. Perhaps exasperation. There was more I could learn here, and I wanted to know what it was. Drake could sense my question.

"Yes, there is a religion on earth that has nothing to do with God."

"*A* religion?"

"I call it a religion. But I mean that in the broad sense of a system of attitudes, beliefs, and practices. I'd say it's not an organized religion, except there are some organized institutions that promote it, and people flock to it. They adhere to this belief system as strongly as some people follow a religion pointed towards God."

My curiosity was piqued. "What religion is it?"

"It's the religion of darkness; the lowest frequencies of hate, envy, and fear. It's a scourge across the entire planet. Its followers can be as fanatically devoted to it as a committed follower of God. They live it, breathe it, preach it to others.

"They seek converts to join them in their philosophy. There are people on earth who benefit from this religion. As long as they can keep drama and fear and loathing in the forefront of people's minds, they can keep the world divided. And if the world is divided—if they can keep turning people against each other—then they believe they are winning. They believe that they are preventing humanity from raising their frequency of love."

"Winning what?"

"The battle against Light. The battle against God. The battle against Love."

"But why would anyone want to do that?"

"Like I said, some creations can be pretty slow sometimes."

"But what can we do about it? I mean, hasn't it always been that way?"

"It doesn't have to be. And the more of you who live by Love and share Light with the world, the more it will touch others and show them the better way. When we love another person unconditionally, we create a connection with them. When we share Light, we are sharing any force that raises frequency. That connection and sharing can help to heal a lifetime of wounds."

"But how do I do that?"

"You start with your own life. Where do you find sources of fear, of shame, of anger, of jealousy, of despising others? Look closely at those areas and recognize that they do not come from God. They are a threat to you and are the opposite of God. Those attitudes and emotions focus only on the mortal conditions in the material world, and the result is like a religion of darkness across the entire world. It's all that some people think about, and it completely replaces any light and love from God."

As I considered his words, I knew he was right, I could see how I had done that very thing. I didn't even realize what it was doing to me.

"So, are we ever justified in being mad at someone?" I asked.

"Mad at the person? Or mad at what they did?"

"I get it."

"Do you?" I knew Drake knew the answer already.

"I think so. God loves everyone, no matter what they do, even if what they do hurts themselves or someone else."

Drake smiled. "You're starting to get it. I'll admit, the concept can be a challenge to master. So many human relationships are conditional. How many times have you heard, 'We were friends until they…' and then there is some explanation as to why the friendship ended. We need to learn to love like God does—unconditionally. What you're fighting against is your ego. Your ego is like weights in the gym. You can either stub your toe on it, or strain yourself against it, or use it carefully and intentionally to make yourself stronger. When you give love, it raises your own frequency, and can also help to raise the frequency of anyone receiving that love."

"So how do I get better at loving everyone?"

"That brings us to the next principle you need to learn."

Chapter 8

LISTEN TO
YOUR INNER VOICE

"YOU WILL PROGRESS FASTER, and will be in closer touch with God, as you learn to listen to your inner voice."

"Do you mean my conscience?"

"Not exactly. Not if you mean your internal sense of right and wrong. Your conscience is definitely important, but that's not what I mean when I talk about your inner voice."

"What is it then?"

"Everyone hears it in their own way, and not always the same way every time. For some people, it can seem like an actual voice."

I suddenly remembered the young medic hearing a voice say, "This man is not dead."

"Other times," Drake continued, "it can seem like a thought

or impression. Your inner voice can seem like it's coming from you, at least until you learn to distinguish the difference between the thoughts you create and those that come to you from elsewhere."

"Where do they come from if not from me?"

"You have probably heard it described as God's Spirit talking to you. That's a close enough explanation."

"But not exactly?"

"No, not exactly. It can also come from those helpers I mentioned earlier, who assist and act on behalf of God." Drake paused for a moment, as if weighing whether I was ready for more. "It's really a little more complex. You see, all truth exists everywhere in the universe. When you tune your mind, your body, and your spirit to the right frequencies, you can tap into divine truths by connecting with your higher self—that part of you that is still directly connected with God. When your whole being is attuned to the right frequency, you can simply ask God and then instantly know the answer."

"I can get the answer to any question?"

Drake smiled. "I know what you're thinking. Again, it's not as simple as it might sound. If you want the answer to something selfish, and ask with selfish intent, then you are already out of alignment. Remember, it all has to do with being in tune with the right frequency. And you also have to remember your reason for being on Earth to begin with."

"To learn?"

"Yes. To learn, to grow, and to exercise that divine ability to choose. It's just as a parent lets a child explore on their own, so they can learn to make their own decisions, but the parent is close by to help if the child gets stuck. Sometimes, it's other family members, or close friends, or mentors who help. They can all contribute to our growth."

I sensed that there was more behind what he was saying. As soon as I had the thought, Drake smiled.

"Yes. There are others who help us and spiritually guide us while on Earth. But there are others who have a calling to be a mentor."

"Like you?"

"My calling is actually a bit different. I'm more of a guide. But yes, there are those who can help provide answers and promptings. You could call them angels. It's an accurate enough name. So, learn to listen to that inner voice."

"How can I get better at that?"

"It takes practice. As you intentionally pay attention to that voice, you can get better at recognizing it and listening to what it tells you. There are other things you can do, too, that will help make you more receptive. Things that will make you a better antenna if you will."

"What are those things?"

"The most basic is to take care of your body. If you don't get enough sleep, you will be less receptive to promptings. It's the same if you get too much sleep. Either way, your body, and your mind, will be sluggish. The things you take into your body make a difference, too."

My thoughts turned to the supplement I had taken. I wondered what had been wrong with it. Drake gave me a knowing look, and I put the thought from my mind, focusing again on the lesson.

"There are so many chemicals in the food you eat these days. Preservatives, artificial colors, artificial flavors. They build up in your system and degrade your spiritual antenna. You can still receive impressions with a damaged antenna, but you're not as receptive as you could be. The closer to the earth your food is, the better it is for your spirit as well as your body."

That made sense to me. "You said that taking care of my body is the most basic way. Are there other ways to improve my… reception?"

"That's our next principle, Vinney."

Chapter 9

USE TECHNOLOGY RESPONSIBLY

"PEOPLE THINK THAT HUMANITY is so advanced. It would be funny if it wasn't so sad. Yes, humans have created a lot of great technology and made great advances in science. But so many people think that all of these achievements mean that they no longer need God. That they have progressed beyond what they think are primitive beliefs. The unfortunate thing is how much truth and power they are actually giving up because they think it has to be one or the other."

"But I still believe in God."

"Which is good, yes. But even then, you still haven't mastered this next principle—the need to put science and technology in its proper place and role. Too many people let technology control their life. For some, it's just a distraction from better things; for others, it's an addiction. They'll watch and listen to things that degrade their spirit without a second thought, never once pausing to ask, 'Should I be watching this?' or 'How is this affecting me?'

"It's possible to allow yourself to be buried so deep in technology, or what technology provides access to, that you can turn off that connection to spiritual things altogether. It can be as powerful as a drug that overrides your ability to reason and choose. When you reach that point, you no longer have a connection to your higher frequency, or to God. You will be left in a lonely, dark void where there are only lower and lower frequencies."

"That sounds bad."

"See for yourself."

We stopped, and I followed Drake's awareness. I became aware of orbs of light in the distance, near the large sphere we were traveling to. They were as large as planets, but I was able to perceive individual people within them and what they were doing. I saw them wandering in dark places, yearning for entertainment. Some people were just staring at their own hands, hoping for a phone to materialize. They were so focused on filling that desire that they were completely unaware of the glorious world filled with light that waited just beyond their perception.

"You see," Drake continued. "Just as what you eat affects your body, the information you take in affects your soul. What you see, what you hear, what you say: all of these things influence the state of your soul when your mortal life is over. Some people will take in anything, and technology just makes it easier to do this all the time."

"So, how do you know what is good and what is bad?"

"Your inner voice can help if you set the technology aside long enough to listen. Focus on developing your higher self, so you have a good, strong communication channel with God. Make sure that your antenna is working well, and that you are paying attention to the messages you receive. If you're distracted all the time, it won't matter what messages come to you because you simply won't notice them."

"That makes sense."

"Understand that technology can be a powerful tool for good. Imagine having access to all of these wonderful tools and using them to enhance your life and enable a closer relationship to God. Don't let technology be a distraction from your spiritual growth. Control it. Put it aside sometimes. Don't sleep near it. Don't reach for it when you first wake up in the morning. Listen to your inner voice and connect with the divine. Develop those things that you can enjoy after you die: great memories, family, friends, your relationships, and your character. All of those things persist."

"What about games, and movies, and distractions like that?"

"Entertainment is okay. Just be aware of what kind of entertainment, and how much of it you are taking in. You can enjoy dessert once in a while, but you wouldn't eat only dessert every meal every day. That would be bad for your body. It's the same for your soul, and, just as there are some things that you should never eat, there are some forms of entertainment that you should never consume. Those things will only harm your soul. Be aware and be wise."

"Right," I said, though honestly, I didn't know how helpful that advice would be to me at the time. After all, I had already left my body behind. "What else do I need to learn?"

Drake smiled. "The next one may surprise you."

Chapter 10

RELEASE PREJUDICE

As WE MOVED CLOSER to the bright sphere in the distance, I felt resistance again. Something new was slowing my progress until I could not move forward.

I looked to Drake. "What's happening?"

"Look deep inside. What do you see?"

I searched my soul and found a darkness there. It wasn't a strong or deep darkness, but it was so deeply ingrained that I didn't even realize it was there. It was holding me back, and I had to let it go if I was to move on.

Prejudice. For the first time, I realized the depth of my prejudice against other human beings. Not enough for me to hate them, but enough to judge and categorize them by simply looking at or hearing them. I was dismayed. Throughout my life, I thought I had been raised to be tolerant and accepting of everyone. I always felt that I was the least prejudiced person I knew, yet, here I was with a dark sliver of prejudice piercing my heart. I was embarrassed, and ashamed. I'd had no idea.

"What do I have to do to get rid of this?"

"Your culture, society, and family have all programmed the weakness of prejudice deep inside of you," Drake explained. "The only way to shed this is to understand the most basic principle of all."

"And that is?"

"God created all life. We are all one—far more than you realize. When we feel dislike, hate, or prejudice towards any of God's creations, we are really directing those energies to our Creator and back to ourselves. To hate or judge anyone is to hate or judge yourself."

"But…" I was still trying to justify my prejudice. I wanted to find some excuse to disapprove of those I didn't agree with, those who hurt me, those who scared me, those who… and then I saw it.

"Prejudice is a form of withholding love, isn't it?"

Drake smiled and nodded. "Now you're getting it. When people have wrong ideas, or do wrong things, you don't have to approve of their actions. I know it's enticing to let that disapproval spread to the person; to make assumptions about them, their values, even their worth and their destiny."

"And we overcome prejudice by focusing on love."

I could sense that my answer pleased him.

"Exactly. When you love someone unconditionally, you see them as they really are. You keep foremost in your mind that they are a child of God. They have a divine nature, even with their flaws. When you see someone as God sees them, all of the labels that you put on them just fade away. That's really all prejudice is: labels. And labels are a mortal weakness."

I searched my heart, striving to root out any prejudicial judgments I had made over the course of my life. The horrific events of September 11, 2001, were still fresh in my memory. I realized how much mistrust I had built up against an entire segment of humanity because of that. I had thought of millions of individual souls in broad terms and attributed the actions of a few to the intentions of each and every one of them.

Drake saw that I was struggling and shared an image with my mind, a cherished memory from my time on Earth. My nephew had just been born, and I was holding him for the very first time. He was so small, so fragile, and so perfect. Here was precious innocence and magnificent potential fresh from the realms of heaven. My heart swelled with joy and couldn't contain the love that I felt for this miracle in my arms.

I felt Drake share in the joy and warmth of that experience. He asked me, "What if your nephew had been born in the Middle East instead of the United States? Would you love him any less?"

"I would love him no matter where he was," I said.

"Even if he had a different skin color? Or was raised with a different set of beliefs from you?"

I thought of the pure love I felt for him as his little hand gripped my finger. "Not one bit."

"And what if he wasn't even your nephew? Would that change his value?"

I tried to consider another answer, just for a fleeting moment, but the love I had for my nephew was too strong.

"No. If I could know him as I knew him when he was born, I would love him no matter what."

"Every single creation is like your nephew. It's only a lack of love that makes you see them in some other way. Prejudice replaces love. It is like an ugly weed that chokes out a beautiful flower. God has no prejudice. You cannot fully return to God while holding on to prejudice."

"But what about people who reject the *truth*?"

Drake gave me a knowing look. "Do you mean those who reject the truth, or those who reject your religious beliefs?"

"But they're the same thing, aren't they?"

I was aware that our progress had completely stopped now, and we floated in the vastness of space. Drake put his arm around me and unfolded an image in my mind as he explained it to me.

"Imagine one hundred people sitting on a bright green hillside with wildflowers in full bloom. It's a bright spring day after a fresh rain. The sun emerges from the clouds and stretches out its rays, creating a perfect rainbow on the far side of the valley. Each of those one hundred people grabs a piece of paper and a pen and starts describing that rainbow. How many different versions of that rainbow will be written down?"

"Probably close to a hundred."

"One hundred. Some will be very similar to each other, but none of them will be exactly the same. But here's the thing: no matter how good the description, no matter how thorough, none of the descriptions can let you fully experience the rainbow. Because the only way you can truly know what the rainbow looks like is to see the rainbow yourself. And the only way to do *that* is through God's love."

"So, religion is like one of those people trying to describe the rainbow?"

"Exactly. There will be a few of those people who are going to describe the rainbow accurately, so if you've never seen a rainbow before, when you do, you will recognize it."

"But then how do teachings that are just plain wrong, descriptions that aren't even part of the rainbow, get into religions?"

"Anywhere you find prejudice in a religion, it is not from God. That is where the work of mortals has crept in. That does not mean that there is no truth to be found in that religion, just that an untrue teaching has taken root, like a weed in the garden. It's easy to confuse culture and truth; it happens all the time. I saw it during my own life on Earth. It could also be from the minds of people who are using their own image to create what they think an ideal world would be."

"How can I recognize the difference?"

"Prejudice only grows from negative emotions, never from positive ones. Any time you find negative emotions—most commonly shame and fear—those are not coming from God. Whenever you find love, that is where you will find God. Where religion influences and guides a soul towards authentically loving every one of God's creations, especially those who are hurting, or different, or suffering from prejudice, that is when religion works to help people raise their frequency."

"And then they can see the truth themselves."

"Exactly. Your primary job in life, regardless of your religion, is to open your heart to God's love, so that you can tell the difference between the words of mortals and the words of God. You can then tell the difference between culture and God's love, and you can choose love."

At that moment, maybe for the first time ever, I truly wanted to release all of the prejudice in my heart and replace it with God's love for everyone. Fortunately, I had been raised by my mother to love everyone, regardless of their background or race, and that had helped to counter much of the cultural influences that had crept into my mind. Still, I had fallen prey to societal influences where I judged many people by the evil actions of a few. I worked to release those prejudices, too.

Through the process, as I invited the light and love of God into me, I noticed another prejudice that the culture I was raised in had programmed into me. I had judged the worthiness of those who lived a different lifestyle, particularly one based on a person's sexuality. Now I understood that, just because someone had a different sexuality than mine, it did not make them in any way less important to God. God loves every single one of us the same. He loves every hair on your head, He loves every skin cell on your body. He loves each and every one of us equally. He doesn't sit there and think, "This is a bad soul." He thinks, "I love this soul. I want to help love this soul through any trial it has."

Many organizations, including some religions, choose to ostracize and push away people because of religion, skin color, sexuality, lifestyle, or their belief systems. That's their prerogative, of course, but that choice is not in accordance with God's will.

It took some time and effort, but I was able to release the last of the prejudice that was holding me back. I let go of all of the labels and replaced them with love. I could feel my frequency elevate to match my love.

Drake gave me a hug, and we resumed our journey to the sphere of light in the distance that loomed larger with each passing moment. I began to discern greens and blues on the surface.

"Is that a planet?" I asked. "Or, is that heaven?"

"Yes, it is a heaven," Drake said. "One of many. It is also a planet."

"So, heaven is an actual physical place, not just spiritual?"

Drake smiled. "Yes, it is a spiritual place, and yes, of course, it is a physical place."

"What exactly is heaven, then?"

"Heaven is a place where souls can go to heal, to learn, and to prepare for further growth."

"And there's more than one?"

"There are as many as God's children need."

Chapter 11

The Power of Creation

"Do you believe in magic?" Drake asked.

"What, like waving wands and saying spells?"

He smiled. "No. That's all storytelling. I'm talking about the essence of the word, its core meaning: having an extraordinary power to influence things in a way that defies mortal explanation."

"Not really."

"Then you don't believe in miracles?"

"Oh, yes. I do. But those aren't magic. Are they?"

"Not in the fantasy storytelling way, no. But there is a power that you can tap into that can seem like magic. Because you have a spark of divinity in you, you can use that spark to exercise the power of creation. In fact, you have that power available in the physical world. On Earth, can you create an entire building?"

"No. All I've ever done is framing and finishing work. I don't know anything about making a whole building."

"You could if you really wanted to."

"I mean, I guess I could. But it would take a lot of time and work, and a lot of skills I don't have now."

"Yes, but you could build a structure. You wouldn't necessarily need to swing the hammer yourself."

"What do you mean?"

"Think about it. You can find an engineer or an architect and have them draft the detailed plans, right?"

"Yes."

"And then you could hire a general contractor. That person would oversee other people doing the construction until the building was finished."

"But I didn't actually build it."

"Are you sure? You may not have made it materialize out of thin air, or even have pounded a single nail. But would that building exist if you did not first envision it? Or if you didn't start the process that led to its completion?"

"I guess not."

"Making things in the physical world takes physical material and physical labor, but before any of that, it begins with a thought—a vision—and a desire to create something. Your thoughts are the first step in creation."

"But that doesn't seem like magic. It's more like work."

"Who said magic doesn't require work?" Drake gave me a wry smile. "Besides, that is just one example and a very basic one. It is possible to create far greater things with far less physical effort."

Drake shared an example of how will and intention exert power over matter. Thoughts operate much like electromagnetic energy, with the brain functioning as an antenna that transmits the instructions to organize and direct it all.

My builder's mind started to take over. "But how does the brain jump that physical barrier into directing matter just by thinking about it?"

Drake smiled patiently. "You don't need to understand how all of it works right now. Just learn the basic principles of creation, and you can put them to use."

"But—"

"Trust me. You don't need to know how a lightbulb works in order to turn on a lamp. For now, understanding the basic principle of clarifying and focusing your intention is enough. Your intention can literally move mountains if it is pure enough and aligned with God."

I had read about such things in the Bible growing up but was never sure if it was literal or metaphorical. It turns out it was literal. "That's amazing."

"Yes, it is. However, the power of creating with your thoughts can also work against you."

"How?"

"If you think about negative things, you will create negative things."

"Even if I don't want to? What if I'm just thinking about something I want to get rid of?"

"It doesn't work that way. Focusing on a thing will only build that thing, whether good or bad. If you want to get rid of something negative, you need to think about what you want to replace it with. Focus on what you want, and it will naturally replace whatever it is you don't want. The good will replace the bad as you make the good grow."

"Is that why it's important to be surrounded by positive things?"

"Exactly. You can train and condition your thoughts in many different ways—the television and movies that you watch, the music you listen to, the books you read, even the people you associate with. You create your environment, which helps to shape your thoughts, which determines what you create in your life."

"But I can't create just any old thing I want, right? I mean, just thinking won't stop bad things from happening."

"What would you consider to be a 'bad thing'?"

"I don't know. Most people would consider dying to be a bad thing."

"Now that you've done it, do you still think it's bad?"

I thought for a moment, then smiled. "No. I guess it isn't."

"Try another one, then. What is something else that could be bad?"

"Losing a job? Getting sick?"

"And why would those things be bad?"

"Because…I don't know. I guess because they're uncomfortable? Because they stop me from getting what I want?"

"Do those things alone stop you, or do you allow yourself to be stopped because you are distracted by the discomfort? You stop focusing on creation and, instead, wallow in doubt and self-pity. You allow your thoughts to turn to negative things instead of staying focused on the positive."

Just then my thoughts turned to the abusive situations I had suffered as a child. I knew he was aware of my thoughts.

"Yes," Drake said. "Sometimes it may feel impossible to see the good in the moment. It may even seem impossible for years afterwards. But that doesn't change your power to choose your perspective."

I didn't want to admit it, but I knew he was right.

"You see, your thoughts can create and transform not only your environment, but also how you experience that environment. Even the worst situations can strengthen you and help you to grow. Once you truly understand that, you may feel down but you'll never feel defeated, even on your worst day. Of course, the opposite is true as well. You can have a seemingly wonderful life, but if you focus long enough on just the bad aspects of life, you will eventually replace all of the good things with bad things, both in your mind and in reality."

"So, my focus is key."

"Yes. Whatever you give your attention to, whatever you focus on, good and bad, you attract and then create into existence. So, be careful what thoughts you hold in your mind. Think about positive things, and you will build positive things, both internally and externally. Dwell on negative thoughts and emotions, and you'll tear down positive things and create negative things in their place, even if your intentions are good. As they say, 'the road to hell is paved with good intentions.'"

I was surprised to hear him say that. "That's a saying here, too?"

Drake laughed. "We more fully understand that concept here than on earth. We know that those in the physical realm allow ego to corrupt even the greatest of intentions. On this side, there isn't the ability to corrupt a good intention because you can't conceal anything. It is simply impossible to lie."

"I need to focus on the good that I want to create."

"Yes. Recognize the magic in your thoughts. Focus on what you want to create. Set your intentions. Then control your actions. That will create your environment, both internally and externally, and that will help you achieve your ultimate potential."

I made the connection with our previous discussion about technology. "And my thoughts are influenced by what I surround myself with."

"Exactly. Speaking of which, let's talk about one of the biggest influences on what people think about and how they see the world."

Chapter 12

AVOID NEGATIVE INFLUENCES

"Do you remember the religion of darkness I mentioned earlier?"

"Yes."

"There are people who preach it constantly. They may not even know they are preaching a religion, but they know that they are feeding on feelings of fear. They design their message around it. They profit and expand their power through it."

"Who are they?"

"They're all around you. You can find them in many places, and in many ways, but the most common is the news."

"You mean the people on the news?"

"No. The news companies themselves. The directors, the editors, the writers, and reporters."

News stories did tend to focus on the bad things happening in the world, I thought.

"But isn't it important to know what is going on in the world?"

"But do you really?"

"Sure. I can learn about what is going on in other countries, natural disasters, and things like that."

"Do you believe that is a clear picture of everything going on? Or is it just the rare and titillating things?"

"Well, it's useful information."

"Useful? What do you do with that information? Does it change how you live your life?"

I had to admit that other than how it made me feel, most of what I heard on the news didn't really affect me at all. It was more interesting than useful.

"Not usually, no. But isn't there any good that can come from it?"

"Of course, but you need to be wise and very selective. It is easy to get pulled into the river of despair and fear of the constant news cycle. It changes how you see the world, the way you think about events and other people. It feeds prejudice and dampens love. Over time, everything will just seem negative, and you will lose touch with the brightness that comes from God."

"Like when you said that everything that we allow inside of us affects us?"

"Exactly. The religion of darkness wants everyone to watch violence, drama, and fearful images every day, all day long. Some people do. If it was up to this religion, there would only be news channels focused on every negative event everywhere.

They don't want people watching positive entertainment. They don't want you to watch anything that builds your inner light or your soul, because when you do that, they lose influence over you."

"But sometimes there are good news stories."

"Sometimes. Understand that news programs are running a business, and they will do everything they can to appeal to base emotions to hook you and keep you coming back for more. Look closely at how even good news stories are constructed; they're laced together with pain, hurt, and negativity. Weaving tension and conflict into the story is how they make it more engaging. Our baser natures are naturally drawn to those lower frequencies."

"So, I should have just avoided the news completely?"

"That's not what I'm saying. You are right that it is good to know what is going on in the world, especially when you can make a difference. Just be aware of the nature of the programs, and limit the attention and energy you give to it. If you're constantly exposed to negativity and pain, over time, they will create a damaged person with a corrupted soul. Maybe not completely broken, but not completely whole, either."

I thought of people I knew who seemed to be addicted to news stories. They either had to have the news running on their TV, or, if they were away from a TV, had to check the news on their phones regularly, afraid that they might be missing something. Drake was right. These people seemed pessimistic, doubtful, or fearful.

"The sad reality about the news is that they are in the business of conflict. They thrive and profit from it. Most of it is designed for entertainment. There are directors, just like in movies and television shows. They can take a molehill and turn it into a mountain. Likewise, they can take a mountain and make it a molehill. They get to script what you see and hear, and, therefore, what you believe. It's more insidious than fiction because you believe that what they are telling you is absolutely true, even though it is filtered and packaged in a way that distorts the real truth. Do not allow them that power over you."

"So, how am I supposed to know what is important or right?"

"Always remember that you're hearing the news second-hand. When you do, and when you are connected to God, you'll know the truth of what stories are important and what stories aren't. You can then seek out those stories that are truly important for you and only expose yourself to those things.

"Learn to ignore the noise—the distractions that keep you angry and fearful and isolated from your brothers and sisters, because that's their ultimate goal."

"Their goal?"

"The goal of the religion of fear. They want you to believe that whatever culture is not your culture is your enemy. They want you to believe that whatever race is not your race is your enemy. They want you to believe that any sexual orientation that is not your sexual orientation is your enemy. That applies to anyone who is different. It applies to people who prioritize values differently. People who think differently. People who make more or less money. People who live a different life or live in a different place or speak a different language. They want us all to be enemies against each other.

"Don't be fooled by stories that are wrapped in good news but are actually full of negative emotions at their core. Even when the news paints a story promoting unity, often the story is structured to exploit the divides between us and to make people think in terms of conflict. If you can find stories that are purely good, by all means take those in. Share them. The world needs more of that. It would make everyone happier and a lot of lives better."

"That makes sense."

"We've mostly discussed the news, but realize, though, that it's not just news organizations. There are plenty of other organizations that also thrive on conflict and exploit divisiveness to gain followers and build support for their cause. Whoever they are, if you follow their teachings, you are out of alignment with God."

"That sounds like politics."

"Yes, political parties are on that list. And there are plenty of other distractions that can get you focused on the wrong things."

"Like what?"

"There is more to come. As earth's technology advances, there will be more ways that people can feed the negative emotions of fear. New technology is coming that will enable people to feed their pride in what they show off to the world, or their envy of what other people are showing off that they don't have.

"You see, the religion of darkness wants you to portray a perfect life to others. Creating that illusion makes you think that you feel better, but it really just leaves you hollow and unfulfilled. Even if you mean for it to inspire others, what you share can leave them feeling jealous and dissatisfied with themselves and their imperfect world."

I suddenly understood the impact of television and movies that portrayed life inauthentically. Even though I knew they weren't showing real life, their stories and messages had definitely influenced my thoughts, desires, and behavior.

Drake gave me a broad smile. "Yes, you are making the connections. Very good."

"But can't the media be used for good?"

"Of course, it can. I'm not saying that media itself is bad. It's just a powerful tool that the religion of darkness uses to mix up emotions and motivations."

"Like the news?"

"Exactly. Between us all there is absolute truth. And it's in that truth that we find commonality. It is in that commonality that we find God, love, and the fundamentals to freedom, power, and true empowerment. Does that make sense to you?"

I nodded. "Yes."

"Good. Now I think you'll find this next principle interesting."

"What's that?"

"Let's talk about the devil."

Chapter 13

THE PURPOSE OF EVIL

"THERE REALLY IS A DEVIL?" I was raised to believe that there was a devil, but, to me, it always felt more like a concept than a being. I knew as soon as I thought the question that he was very real.

"He goes by many names," Drake said. "Satan. Lucifer. Ác Quỷ. Alshaytan. I'll call him the devil, since that is what you know him by."

"What purpose does he serve?" I asked. "Why would God allow the devil to have so much influence over us?"

Drake reflected for a moment, then said, "Let's use something you're already familiar with to illustrate the point."

An image filled my mind. Two teardrop shapes curved into each other, one white, the other black. I recognized it as the symbol of yin and yang. I was surprised. "Is that a sacred symbol?"

Drake looked amused by the question. "No, but it is useful to teach a truth. Tell me what you see."

"I see a light shape and a dark shape turning into each other."

"Right. And what do you see inside each of those shapes?"

"There is a white circle inside the dark shape, and a dark circle inside the white shape."

"Right again. Inside every dark experience is the potential for light, learning, and growth. You can take every bad thing that ever happens to you and use it to make the light within you stronger."

"And the dark circle inside the white shape?"

"What do you think it means?"

"That we can take even the brightest experiences and turn them dark somehow?"

"Correct. We'll talk about that more in a moment. First, understand that all of us have the capacity for darkness, if we let ourselves be influenced by the devil instead of by God, and even the worst of us still has that spark of divinity within. We all have the capacity for redemption, for forgiveness, and for God's love. No matter how far we think we've fallen, or how lost we may be, He will always welcome us back if we nurture that light and turn to Him."

"But why does He want us to have that struggle to begin with? Why not just let us experience good without all of the bad?"

"You're into physical fitness, right? Building your body and growing stronger?"

"Yes." I tried to not be distracted by the fact that the reason I was even here with Drake was because I drank something that I thought would help me get stronger but poisoned me instead.

"What do you have to do to build your muscles?"

"Lift weights, mostly."

"Exactly. You use resistance. Something for your muscles to work against. Why do you do that?"

"Without resistance, the muscles won't get stronger."

"Isn't that uncomfortable?"

"Sure, but it's worth it."

"In what way?"

"I'm stronger. I can do more. I feel healthier."

"Exactly. It's the same with our spirit. The only way for us to grow stronger is to face resistance. If our spirit was put into an existence where everything was easy, we would never learn anything."

I thought back to the darkness in my childhood. There was a lot of it. Fear. Pain. I grew up creating an alternate universe in my mind where I was safe. Now, I could clearly see that despite all of the darkness—or, perhaps, precisely because of it—those experiences had shaped me into the person I was. And I wouldn't have changed a thing. Not a single day, not a single moment, not a single instance of pain or hurt that was done to me.

I knew that I was right where God wanted me to be. I didn't want to change His plans for me as He molded me into who I was. If I hadn't experienced that darkness, I didn't know if the light would have grown in me.

I realized that, even in our darkest days, we should remember that there is still light. We are never truly alone. Ever. And we need to be aware that when we are full of light, living in the light side of that image, there is still darkness trying to creep in.

Drake let those thoughts sink in before he continued.

"You said a moment ago that we can take even the brightest experiences and turn them dark."

"Yes."

"Darkness. Fear. That is the nature of the devil. When we were in God's presence before coming to Earth, we couldn't make a wrong choice."

"We existed before we were born on Earth?"

"We did." Drake shared an image of a sky-blue ribbon that stretched infinitely in both directions, beyond the edges of the universe he had shown me when we first met. I noticed a single grain of sand, glowing bright gold, resting on the ribbon in front of me.

"The ribbon represents your eternal existence," Drake said. "The grain of sand represents your time on Earth. Your mortal experience is a brief event that provides essential opportunities for learning and development. Before coming to Earth, awash in God's love, the idea of a wrong choice couldn't even enter our minds."

"So, there was no resistance?"

Drake nodded. "Which means there was also no growth. Living on Earth is like going to a spiritual gym to develop and strengthen our spirit and character—the very core of who we are."

"And the devil creates that resistance?"

"Yes, he works against us doing the right thing. Or he influences us to do the right thing, but with the wrong motivation. Both are harmful to our growth."

"What do you mean?"

"Every decision we make is motivated by either fear or joy. I'm simplifying it, but that's pretty much what everything comes down to. When we truly understand God's love for us, there is nothing to fear. We especially shouldn't fear failure. Mistakes and failures are a necessary part of our progress. God knows we're going to fail, just as a child learning to walk stumbles and falls, but He loves us completely and unconditionally. Whenever we do something that is motivated by fear, our frequency moves down, even if the outcome is good."

"My frequency can fall even if I'm doing what I'm supposed to? Even if I'm doing the right thing?"

"That's right. The devil and his followers motivate through fear. Realize that in the mortal existence, you can only receive mortal benefits when following the devil's influence: money, fame, influence over others. If you pursue them through the devil's path, any benefit will end with your mortal life."

"What do you mean?"

"Say, you want money. You could follow the devil's prompting and rob a bank, or you could follow God's influence and learn how to earn that same amount of money. Once you have learned how to earn that money, you can repeat that success over and over again. You will have learned how to grow instead of destroy, and that knowledge is powerful, because everything you learn remains with you after you die."

"That makes sense."

"No matter what drives you, it's always worth following the path of light. You have that choice in every moment of decision. Whenever you do anything out of selfless love, that is a connection with God. It's the highest motivation you can have. It's the best reason for doing anything. It elevates you and your frequency. For example, say you haven't taken care of your body. Fear of sickness might be what initially motivates you to change, but you then need to set your intention towards what you want—in this case, good health—not what you don't want. Focus on the love and gratitude you have for the gift of your body, and your desire to treat it well."

As I thought back on the reasons that I had done things throughout my life, I could see that what he was saying was true. Whenever I did something out of fear, even if I was doing the right thing, I didn't feel the same as when I did it out of love. Whenever I acted out of love, I felt stronger and more fulfilled.

"I think we've talked about this enough. Just remember that the devil's job is to influence you to make decisions that pull you away from God. His job plays a vital role in your progress. Recognize his temptations, so that you are empowered to make a clear choice. Act with love, not fear."

I thought I was ready to move on, but I hesitated. I could feel the resistance to movement again. Drake paused and waited for me to work through my thoughts.

I had an uncle who was an atheist. He was a kind and loving man, but he refused to believe in God. He said it was because he couldn't believe that a good being would allow so much pain and suffering in the world. Even though I believed in God, I could feel that my love for my uncle had imprinted some of his beliefs on my psyche. I was stuck, and I didn't know what to do.

Drake followed my thoughts, then said, "I know that it can all seem very unfair while you're on Earth."

"Not just *unfair*," I said. "There are horrific things that happen to good people on Earth. Some of the worst things imaginable happen to innocent little children. Why does it have to be that way?"

"Remember that the purpose of life is to learn and to grow, and the only way to do that is to experience opposition, struggle, even pain and anguish. And yes, there are great evils that are perpetrated on innocent people. It is not their fault. Sometimes, it is because others use their agency for evil. Other times what appears like a random accident was an experience chosen by that person before they even came to Earth, for their own benefit, and the benefit of others."

"But how does that explain a child that dies of cancer, or a newborn that dies after only a few hours? Are you saying they chose that path? How does being here such a short time benefit them?"

"On Earth, so much is defined by time, but time is not an absolute measure of growth. For some, all it takes is a brief moment in mortality to bring about powerful changes. Think of it like a caterpillar, which must go through the chrysalis stage to become a butterfly. It is only in the chrysalis for a short span of its existence, but the transformation turns it into a completely new creature that can do far more than it could as a caterpillar."

"And mortality is like the chrysalis for us?"

"Exactly. Those who are on Earth for a very brief time receive everything that they need from mortality, and, at the same time, play a part in the struggle and growth of those who remain. The same is true for those born with mental and physical disabilities; they have their own path for growth, and they provide opportunities for others to grow as well. Every path is unique, which makes it difficult to provide a simple answer that completely covers every circumstance."

I thought about all of the suffering I had seen and experienced while on Earth.

"I know," Drake said, "that it is difficult to fully understand or believe when the pain feels so intense and all you can see is the short span of your mortal life. Know this, though—every individual is known and completely loved by God. Everyone will experience exactly what they need in this life to progress as much as they can. The suffering will always make sense when you can see the eternal view again."

"But isn't there another way?"

"What would you propose? Something easier? Something that didn't stretch your faith as much? Something that didn't compel you to feel great depths of compassion for others?"

I remembered the image of the yin and the yang. Evil and good in an endless cycle, one growing out of the other.

"I understand," Drake continued. "I know that in the middle of all of the confusion and anguish, it can all seem so very unfair. Life is challenging by design. The sword despises the blacksmith until it is time for battle. Even knowing that there is a greater purpose to the struggle and suffering may not lessen the pain of the experience. But remember how you felt when we first met. In that moment, you were filled with a crushing despair. Fear. Pain. But then you felt... what?"

"Love. Kindness. Tenderness."

"And what happened as soon as you let that light in?"

"All of the negative feelings disappeared. It was like they were never there."

"It's good to feel compassion for others when they are suffering. It's even better to provide love, kindness, and tenderness to them when they need it. It is only through the struggle and challenges that we grow stronger. Just know that no matter how painful it is, the pain does end, and it is all worth it." He smiled. "Come, there's something you should see."

We were now very close to the massive sphere of light. Brilliant white light still emanated from the orb itself, but the white transitioned to blue light as it radiated away from the surface. Then the blue light became purple, and then a misty pink hue before fading away.

As we came nearer, I could see an aura of white light surrounding the planet like a wide belt. Then I saw that the aura appeared to be made of millions, perhaps billions, of small stars, luminous like glowing pearls.

Drake directed my gaze to one of the smaller stars that made up the aura. As I drew nearer, I saw that it was actually made up of points of light. As I looked closer still, I realized that the individual lights were angelic beings arrayed to form a sphere.

I call them angels, as that is the best description of their appearance. They didn't have wings, but they exuded power and glory. They didn't appear male or female, though they had aspects of both. They were handsome and beautiful and powerful and tender and firm and kind and, most of all, glorious.

The angels were all turned inward towards the center of their sphere. I became aware that they were surrounding groups of souls, like a pod. The number of souls in each pod varied;

some held a few souls and others, thousands. I was aware that each pod had a frequency; the souls in each pod shared the same frequency, and often shared the same culture or period in history on Earth, some pods thousands of years ago. I followed Drake's guidance to observe one soul in one pod.

I saw a man with a bushy mustache who I guessed had lived in the early 1900s. He wore brown pants with suspenders, a white undershirt, laced dark brown shoes, and a brown bowler hat. He appeared to be in his thirties or forties, but I somehow knew that he was actually in his sixties when he died.

Most of all, he was angry. Very angry. He shouted in what I recognized as Italian. I understood everything he was saying even though I don't know Italian. I understood who he was, his past, and why he was so angry. He thought he was yelling at his son, or someone who was like a son to him, but there was no one there. He was saying the cruelest and most hurtful things he could think of.

His son had shot or stabbed him, and it took this man a week to die. Even though he had died nearly a century before, he was still shouting and swinging his fists, doing everything he could to harm the imaginary being in front of him with as much violence and anger as he could muster.

Suddenly, it was as if he woke out of a trance as the last of his anger left him. He became aware that he was surrounded by angels. As he looked up and saw them, two angels rushed to his side to embrace him, and he began to cry. In a flash, the three of them began moving towards the large sphere of light. They moved so fast that it looked to me like they simply disappeared, though I instinctively knew where they had gone.

I saw that the souls in each pod were dealing with their own issues: hate, resentment, prejudice, bigotry, addiction. These poor souls were stuck in a loop, like a vinyl record caught on a scratch, skipping over and over.

What was especially sad to me was that these dark souls were surrounded by these glorious beings full of light and love just waiting to help them, but they were so caught up in their own negativity and pain that they weren't even aware of them. All they could do was imagine other souls that they wanted to hurt. It wasn't until they finally let go of that negative energy that they could see the beauty all around them and progress in their existence.

Drake pulled my awareness back, and we resumed our journey. I noticed a large group of angels descending on one of the pods, giving reinforcements to the angels that were already there. I couldn't see inside that pod and didn't know what was happening.

"What is going on there?" I wondered. "Is there a problem?"

Drake smiled with radiant joy. "Not at all. Loved ones are praying for the souls in that pod. Their prayers are granting more power to help cleanse the negative energy they are carrying. Those angels are coming to help that group move on. Groups tend to move up together. Much like a graduation, if you will."

I thought of eggs in a nest, which all tended to hatch about the same time.

Drake heard my thought and smiled. "Yes, like that, too."

Chapter 14

WE ARE ALL ONE

We passed through countless spheres around the central orb of light. It shone with a radiance like Earth's sun, only more brilliant and bright.

Drake continued my lessons. "Fear is the foundation of negative thoughts and emotions. It leads to pride, jealousy, and hypocrisy. It's surprising how many people claim to follow God, or who actually believe that they are following God, but their hearts are far from the love He holds for each and every one of His creations. It's especially sad when those people look down on others who are also trying to draw closer to God but are following a different religion. That's when these pseudo-religious people are some of the biggest hypocrites."

"What do you mean?"

"Do you remember earlier when we talked about how it's like people sitting on a hillside, trying to describe a rainbow?"

"Yes."

"All the descriptions, no matter how accurate or complete, will have truth in them. All of them are valuable as they help people understand and appreciate the rainbow. No matter what name a person calls God, they can connect to God and find absolute, eternal truths, regardless of their religion. God reaches out to all who reach out to Him."

"So, there's truth in all religions?"

"All religions that teach love and encourage you to draw closer to God, yes. That is the most important thing anyone can do. That is the whole purpose of our existence on Earth: to learn, to grow, and to make choices that bring us closer to God."

"But if one religion has more truth than another one, shouldn't everyone go where there is the most truth?"

"Not all truths will resonate with all people; they need a different description to even begin to comprehend the beauty of it all. It is far better for them to draw closer to God in a way that works for them. Most people are in a religion they were born into. If they only stay because they are afraid of being ridiculed, shunned, or disowned, they will progress more slowly."

"So different religions are actually pointed towards the same goal?"

"God is constantly reaching out to His children, and He will meet them whenever and wherever they reach out to Him. Think of it this way: each religion is an island in a chain of islands. People on one island point across the water to another island and say 'They're bad. The way we live is the only true way to live.' The people on the other island are pointing back and saying the same thing. What they don't see is that the same bedrock supports and connects them, and what lies beneath the surface is far, far greater than what they can see above the water. Imagine if all of the religions worked together to bring everyone closer to God, without tearing each other down or resorting to fear as a motivator."

"That would be pretty amazing, actually."

Drake smiled. "It would. Imagine if Buddhism, Christianity, Hinduism, Islam, Judaism, and all of the others worked in cooperation instead of competition. Sometimes they do, or at least try to. But within each one, there are factions that struggle against each other. Here, I want to show you something."

Drake gestured towards another sphere of light. As soon as my attention went to it, my consciousness went there, too. I saw an entire realm of religious people. I could immediately sense the goodness that they had in their hearts, but they were removed from God.

"Why are they here instead of with God?" I asked.

"Look closer. What do you see?"

I looked deeply at them and saw what was keeping them from heaven. I could see, or sense, that there were other people in heaven that the people before me would have nothing to do with; they would never allow themselves to be in the same place as "those heathens" or "those sinners."

"So," I asked, "they are keeping themselves out of heaven?"

"They are. The self-righteous judgment that they are passing on other people is really against them, and only affects them. Remember this: The judgments that you pass on others will keep you from the light and love of God.

"If you find yourself judging another, it's because you're holding a weakness or an insecurity in your own soul. Let go of that insecurity. Release it to God. Let Him strengthen you where you have weaknesses. As He strengthens you, you'll realize that when you're looking at people and seeing what God sees—the children of God in beautiful colors, in beautiful religions, in beautiful lifestyles—you will see that they are all loved beyond measure, and you will glory in the good actions of these creations, regardless of their differences."

Seeing these otherwise "good" people keep themselves from greater happiness because they couldn't overcome their own prejudice filled me with sorrow. I remembered on Earth the times I had seen religious men and women stand by as others were persecuted, ridiculed, and had their freedoms and rights threatened or taken away.

I understood that was not God's way. God created us with free agency, and that anyone who wanted to take away that agency—that ability to choose their own way—was not following God's relationship with his children. It was the opposite of God's way.

As I accepted this with all of my heart, we traveled the final distance towards the glorious sphere ahead of us.

Chapter 15

EXPLORING HEAVEN

AS WE APPROACHED THE SPHERE, I felt like I was immersed in the light of pure love and felt full of peace and joy. That's the only way I can explain it. I also understood that all forms of light—physical, spiritual, and mental—come from God's love.

The realm was brighter than Earth's sun, and, for a time, the light was so bright that I couldn't see anything. I wondered how amazing our own sun would feel if we didn't have a physical body and could just wade into it.

As we entered the realm's upper atmosphere, my vision cleared. I could see that the place was a planet, like Earth, yet, the light that shone from it was actually made up of an infinite spectrum of colors that rippled and flowed, more than my mind could comprehend.

I can't even begin to describe how amazing it was to see so many colors. I thought, just seeing these colors alone would be life changing. Even more astounding was that I could not just see a color—I could *feel* it. Every color has a particular frequency in love, and I could feel that frequency as I experienced the color.

As we descended onto the world through the colors, I felt like I was being loved by a million little kisses. I felt a giddiness in my gut. The first color I picked out was a kind of blue, the brightest, most pristine blue you could ever imagine, bright as neon. Unlike Earth, where the blue sky surrounds us from above, this blue radiated from the world itself. I got the sense that I was seeing the real Earth, and that the one I had been living on was just a copy of this grand planet, a shadow that existed in a lower plane.

I was so caught up in all I was experiencing that I didn't notice that we were about to touch down. It wasn't until I felt the warm, soft grass under my feet that I was aware that we had arrived, and a new kind of sensory experience rippled through me. I could feel the sweet smell and taste of the grass through my toes. I looked down and was overwhelmed by the beautiful, luminous green that radiated from within each blade of grass.

As my wonder and appreciation flowed from me to the grass, I was amazed that the grass reciprocated, sending the same feelings back to me. It wasn't simply a reflection of my own emotions: I was actually communicating with the grass. It had a complex consciousness, an awareness of me and my experience.

"How are you so complex?" I thought.

"We are all individuals," came its response.

Each blade of grass was an individual entity, yet joined

together to create one beautiful, powerful organism. I noticed a buzzing hum as each blade harmonized with its neighbors to create a soft loving frequency that enveloped me.

I immediately absorbed the lesson of the grass: we are each an individual consciousness, individual frequencies, yet, when we act as one body, we have far more power and strength in God.

I asked Drake, "Is my family one of these groups like this grass?"

"Some of you are."

"Why not all of us?"

"Not all of you want to be that way, and that's okay. Some are coming together in a group of love. Some want to be above that frequency, and some want to be below it. Each of us chooses the frequency we are most comfortable with."

I turned my attention back to the grass, lost in the wonder of it all.

"You know," Drake said, "there's a lot more here than just grass."

I pulled my consciousness away from the grass, anxious for more. "Where?"

Drake gestured to a row of flowers beside the field of grass.

I thought, "I would love to experience that flower over there," and immediately my consciousness experienced all the sensations of the flower with absolute love and appreciation. It sent those same powerful feelings right back to me.

As I interacted with the flower, I discovered that it was even more complex than the grass, and the sound emanating from it was even more beautiful than that created by the grass. I could still hear the grass, and the two sounds interacted together in a holy harmony, penetrating every spiritual cell of my being. I wished that everyone could spend just five minutes experiencing a flower in heaven; it would radically change their perception of the universe and their place in it.

Drake held his presence back while I absorbed the sensations around me and basked in the wonder of it all. It was almost too much when he leaned in again and said, "Be careful trying to understand everything all at once. It can overwhelm you."

"Okay," I said, dragging myself back from the glorious edge of amazement.

"Are you ready for more?" I could feel his joy in sharing my wonder of discovery.

"What else is there?"

"There's water."

"Water?" I discovered that I could sense where things were, even if I couldn't see them. I suddenly saw the wider landscape and was in awe at its grandeur. I always had a deep appreciation for nature. As a child, almost every weekend, my family would go to a cabin in Provo Canyon near our home. I loved all forms of nature, and here, before me, it was in its perfect form.

Fields of flowers shone in a myriad of colors. At the edge of these fields, a majestic forest stretched endlessly into the distance. Marking the border between the forest and field, there was a wide stream. I could sense that the stream eventually joined a river, and that river flowed into a large body of water resting deep in the forest beyond my view.

I wanted to experience the stream, and immediately, that's where my awareness was. I plunged headlong into the flow of energy. It was as if every molecule of the water was like a miniature sun. It felt like I had put my head into an earthly stream of water, but it carried a soothing warmth, like the warmth I felt when Drake first appeared in the hospital, but at an even higher level than I had already experienced. It washed away all fear, doubt, and concern. The water had its own music, a melodic flow that rose and fell in sweet healing tones.

I learned that the water existed in appreciation of the love of God. It was like a representation of the love that God has for us and a symbol for the flow of love's energy.

In a millisecond of my experience with the water, I learned how God flows past obstacles. When water encounters an obstacle, it looks for a way around until it finds one, and then it flows around it, surrounding it. It never tires, always seeking to do its work.

I noticed a root in the water. Curious, my consciousness followed the root, which led into a tree. The tree's music flowed easily, and it taught me its lesson: to flow and be open to the flow of life. I learned that trees are as fluid as water. If you were to watch a time lapse film of a seed growing to a sapling to a full-grown tree, you would see its fluidity. If you hammer a nail into a tree, it grows around the nail. Trees can grow around boulders and buildings. A tree can wrap its limbs around anything.

When you encounter an obstacle, don't waste time feeling bad about the obstacle. When a door shuts in front of you, seek to find the new path.

"Did you notice the beetle?" Drake asked.

"Beetle?" I followed his thought back to the flowers. Sure enough, crawling across one of the flowers was a beetle, similar to but more glorious than any beetle on our shadow earth. It looked like a scarab beetle, but was patterned like a bee, with iridescent yellow and blue stripes. I didn't sense any other beetles nearby, and I was aware that it had a more simple, singular consciousness than the networked consciousness of the grass, the flowers, and the tree. I mused that was probably because it was by itself, while the others were part of a network that elevated each individual member.

As I gazed at the beetle crawling across the flower, I could feel that it was tickling the flower, helping it to grow and blossom even more brightly than it had before. I saw the divine nature of this insect and understood that even our smallest influence can serve a divine purpose.

I was still aware of the music from the grass and the flower and the water and the tree, and now the beautiful accents of the beetle layered on top of them, like sprinkles across the icing on a cake. Together they formed a soft, subtle symphony that made my heart swell with gratitude and joy. My happiness was overflowing, and I began to feel like I might just explode from it all.

"Okay, let's bring you back in," Drake said, laughing at my excitement. He reached out his energy and reeled my awareness back into my being as if I were a fish on a line. My energy stabilized, and I regained control of myself, though the wonder of it all was still strong.

Drake gestured to a building on the top of a large hill and said, "Everything here has a frequency. Even buildings like that one."

As my awareness expanded, I noticed for the first time that we were standing in a valley, with a hill rising on one side.

Beyond the hill, the terrain rose ever higher until it became a mountain, more massive than any mountain I had ever imagined. Its snow-covered peak was jagged like the Matterhorn, but larger, with a massive base, as if the Matterhorn had been placed atop Mount Fuji.

On the crest of the hill stood a magnificent white building, five stories tall with a flat roof. The top floor extended outward from the structure, forming a covered porch that was supported by broad fluted columns adorned with intricate scrollwork. Archways on the outer wall reached from the ground halfway up the structure. The building stretched for what seemed like miles, but I couldn't see how far. I just knew that I was seeing just one end of this great building perched on top of the hill.

As I started to focus on the building, the environment's symphony faded into the background of my awareness. I sensed that this building was a place of learning. I noticed a halo of light around the building, and movement around the base.

"Are those people?" I wondered, and instantly my awareness zoomed in and was at the building, amongst the people I had seen from a distance.

The people were walking around, laughing, and hugging each other. Some held hands, but all of them were holding either clipboards, papers, books, or scrolls. They were all excited about whatever it was they were studying.

As a craftsman, my curiosity was drawn back to the building. The building itself looked like it had been made out of a single piece of marble, like a gigantic statue. I was puzzled as I noticed that there were no doors anywhere. There were places where the walls seemed thinner, like translucent windows, and welcoming light radiated from the windows. I couldn't clearly see through the windows, but I could see people were moving around inside. It was like looking through frosted glass or river ice.

"How was this constructed?" I wondered. "How do people get in and out?"

I watched as two people approached the building. I felt their frequency match the frequency of the building, and the building wall rippled and shifted, forming a portal for the two people to enter. As soon as they passed through, the wall flowed closed again. Moments later, I saw others exit the building: the wall simply parted to make a way for them to pass through, and then sealed again. It would glisten and change colors in a reflection of the love and passion of the people entering. It was truly magical.

I knew that even the building had a consciousness, an intellect, and even love. Somehow, this marble structure radiated unconditional love for the students. It knew that it contained great knowledge, and it rejoiced in its ability to share that knowledge with anyone who was ready. All a person had to do was attune themselves to the same frequency of love that the building sent out, and they could enter and share in the joy of learning. I felt its invitation to raise my frequency so that I could resonate with this hall of learning and go inside.

Perhaps the most peculiar thing I had noticed since I arrived was that everything I had encountered had a consciousness. *Everything* was alive. That's when it dawned on me that all the individual consciousnesses that I could feel—from the grass, the flowers, the water, the tree, the insect, and the building—were actually extensions of God.

Before I could speak, Drake said, "Yes, that is correct. You have a piece of that God consciousness inside of you, too. It's what keeps your spirit alive. You were created by God, and everything, both in the physical existence and in the spiritual existence, were all created by God. It was all done out of love. He created a system for us to be able to discover Him in our mortal lives in small and simple ways. Through our mortal experience, we can recognize the unconditional love He has for us."

Drake then drew my awareness back to where we had first touched down. This was the *real* world. Even the most beautiful parts of Earth seemed no more than a pencil sketch compared to the brilliance of this realm.

We stood there together, the soft grass under our feet, a symphony of God's creations in the background of my awareness. I had never been so full of joy.

Then I felt a change in Drake's emotions.

"Vinney," he said with both tenderness and resolution. "I know this is going to hurt, but it will be worth it. I promise." He reached out his energy and embraced me in what I can only describe as a "heart hug."

And then I heard my brother Tyler's voice.

PART III

Chapter 16

MY IRONIC TRAGEDY

I COULD HEAR THE VOICE of my brother speaking from the physical world, as if he was speaking directly into my ear. He was saying a special prayer—what we called a "blessing" in my religion—over my body in the hospital. He stated that I would become whole, and that I would come back.

As he completed the blessing with an "amen," something that felt like a lasso of energy wrapped around me and pulled me back. All of the progress I had made, the incalculable distance I had traveled, disappeared in an instant as I was pulled back into my body.

My brother's blessing was pronounced at 9:30 p.m. on Monday, January 20th. Tuesday morning at 1:11 a.m. I woke from my coma. Drake was right about it hurting. I felt like I was bound in a straitjacket.

Acting on instinct, I ripped off the sensors attached to my

body, pulled the tube out of my throat, and yanked free from the electrodes attached to my head. I ripped off my hospital gown trying to free myself. Then I realized what was causing my feeling of constraint: it was my body.

It is difficult to fully describe the depth or pain of the transition. I was suddenly uncomfortably aware of the cacophony around me. The machines in the room blared alarms. I got out of bed and unplugged the machines to make the noise stop, then grabbed the hospital gown and wrapped it around my waist.

I ran out of the room and down the hallway. At the end of the hall was an elevator. I frantically pushed the elevator button. I didn't know where I was going, and I didn't care. I just had to get out. I was pressing the elevator down button over and over when I saw a nurse walk into my room. She didn't see me at the far end of the hall. *What is taking this elevator so long?* I thought.

The nurse shouted, "Doris!"

Another nurse walked to the room. She gasped in surprise.

I somehow had an awareness of what was going on in my room. The first nurse was looking under the bed and around the room, trying to find where her coma patient had gone.

Doris stepped back out of the room and looked up and down the hallways. I wondered, *Can I run down the stairs? I don't even know where the stairs are. She's going to find me!"*

Then Doris looked straight at me. I had one hand on the elevator button and the other holding the hospital gown around my waist. Doris screamed a full-throated horror movie scream. I almost dropped the gown.

The other nurse ran out of my room, and the two women ran down the hallway towards me. I thought about running again, but I could feel their worry, and I knew that they could get in trouble if I left. Out of respect for them, I couldn't leave. I let them escort me back to my room.

The doctor and the senior nurse on duty arrived shortly after I returned to my room, and I had to answer a battery of questions.

"What happened to you?" the doctor asked. He was shorter than me, perhaps in his mid-fifties. He scrutinized me through thick-lensed glasses.

"I don't know."

I could sense that he was upset, and that nothing about my situation made sense to him. He was trying to figure out how this could have happened. He barely waited for a response before firing the next question at me.

"Do you know the date?"

"No."

"You've been unconscious for three days. Do you know your name?"

"Vinney Tolman." I got that one right.

"Do you know your birth date?"

"September seventh." I got that one right, too.

"Do you know the year you graduated high school?"

"'96." I was on a roll.

"What year is it?"

As the questions continued, the nurses attempted to reconnect me to the sensors and devices, but I ripped everything off almost as fast as they could reattach it. I couldn't stand the feel of anything against my skin. They pleaded with me to cooperate, and we finally settled on a truce with a blood pressure cuff on my right arm, and two sensors on my hand.

They also wanted to give me oxygen since my levels were low when I was in the coma, but the oxygen sensors indicated that my levels were back to normal, so they gave up that fight.

"Look, I just want to go home," I said.

"That's really not a good idea," the doctor insisted. "I'd like you to meet with a neurologist and cardiologist."

The doctor turned to a young nurse in pink scrubs and gave her instructions for a full battery of blood work and other tests. I had never seen her before, but in that moment, I knew that she had a toddler at home. For the first time, I realized that I knew things that I had no reason to know.

"I just want to go home," I repeated, but no one seemed to be listening to me anymore.

By the time the doctor was done giving orders to the nurse, a man in a hospital security uniform arrived to make sure I wasn't going to run again. He hung around the door for a couple of hours then wandered off without a word, apparently satisfied that I was no longer a flight risk.

I kept pushing my call button to ask the nurses how soon I would be able to leave. I couldn't see any reason to stay in the hospital. They told me that my release was not their decision and deferred any discussions about my discharge to the doctor.

When the doctor finally returned, he said, "We'd really like to keep you for another day or two, just to make sure you're really okay."

"No, thank you. I really want to leave."

The doctor sighed and shook his head. "We'll need you to sign release forms."

"I'll sign anything as long as it gets me out of here."

The nursing staff quizzed me for several more hours, asking much the same type of questions as the doctor earlier: What was my address? Where was I born? Which high school did I attend? It seemed as if they were trying to catch me in a contradiction to prove that I wasn't fit to go home. Then they ran me through an MRI scanner one more time, which made me feel especially claustrophobic, even though it only scanned my head.

At the 5:00 a.m. shift change, a neurologist walked into my room.

"Here's my miracle boy," he said. He was clearly in awe of me. "There's really no explanation as to why you're alive, or why you still have a brain that works. You should be dead, or at least a vegetable. It's an absolute miracle."

I didn't know any of that. I remembered nothing after going to my buddy Rob's house. I couldn't even remember going to Dairy Queen. It was like I had a black hole of memory: I knew that there was something there, but I had no idea what it was. After the next hour, I had a steady stream of visitors, with one doctor or nurse after another coming in to see the guy who had died, was in a coma for three days, and was now perfectly healthy as if nothing had happened.

Finally, a little after 6:00 a.m., the doctors and neurologist signed off on my discharge. After signing nearly forty forms, I checked myself out of the hospital. A nurse called my father and arranged for him to drive me home. Honestly, he wasn't my first choice for a ride. My father and I weren't close. We hadn't been for years.

An hour later, I was sitting in a wheelchair in the hospital lobby, waiting for my ride. A tall, lanky orderly stood behind me, his hands gripping the wheelchair handles. My family had taken my personal possessions home while I was in a coma, so all I had to wear was a set of hospital-green scrubs that one of the orderlies gave me. The shirt fit well enough, but the pants were a little tight. I shifted uncomfortably in the wheelchair and slid my feet deeper into the hospital slippers.

When I saw my dad drive into the pick-up lane in front of the main entrance, I felt a pit in my stomach. I didn't expect sympathy from him, or even relief that I was alive. All I expected was a ride home, and maybe some awkward questions I didn't want to answer. I stood up from the wheelchair, thanked the orderly, and walked outside.

My father pulled up to the curb and, without even killing the engine, reached across the passenger seat and pushed open the door. I silently climbed into the car and shut the door. We were on the road home when my dad finally broke the silence. "Are you okay?"

"Yeah." I didn't know what else to say.

"Are you *going* to be okay?"

"Yeah."

"Are you going to work today?" The question didn't surprise me, coming from my dad.

"I don't think so."

"Are you going to work tomorrow?"

"Probably." I didn't see a reason not to. "How's Rob?" I asked.

"They said he's fine. They pumped his stomach."

That was the extent of our conversation. I found out later that my mother had been out of town caring for a relative and didn't even know that anything had happened to me. Apparently, my dad and brother were waiting to see if I was going to live or die before telling her. I went back to work the next day.

───※───

I showed up at work on Wednesday, not sure how my boss, Larry Gleim, would react to my return. No one had told him where I was. Larry was a hard worker. Even in his sixties, he could out-work just about any one of his employees on his construction team.

I walked onto the job site and sought him out. He turned his head in my direction and looked at me through his thick-framed glasses.

"Oh, you're still alive." He said sardonically. "No call and no show for two days. I thought you were dead."

"I was," I said.

"What?" He wasn't sure if I was joking or not.

"If I still have a job, I'll tell you about it."

He didn't hesitate. "Of course, you have a job. We have work to do."

Other than what I'd heard from others, I really didn't have much to tell him. I did tell him about waking up in the hospital, and I showed him where the paramedic made the incision for the tracheotomy.

───※───

Several days later, I went out to dinner at Wingers in Orem with my brother and his girlfriend, my older sister Tami, and her two children. As dinner was winding down, Tami pulled me aside.

"Do you remember anything about dying?" she asked.

Consciously, my thoughts were, *no, nothing happened*, but her question triggered a flood of memories. It was like a computer file hidden deep on a hard drive had been opened, and the information popped up onto the screen of my mind.

The words spilled out. I told her about my spirit guide. I explained to her that I had to be educated in order to return to where we come from, and my guide had taught me what I needed to know. I told her that I had seen heaven; that it was an actual place.

As the words flowed, so did my emotions. Standing in the middle of the restaurant, tears streamed down my cheeks. But even as I told her about what happened after I died, there was a battle going on inside my brain. *Am I crazy? Did I really experience that or did my brain just make it up?*

At first, Tami acted surprised. And a little skeptical. When I finished my story, all she said was, "That makes sense." She had decided that my experience aligned with what she expected to happen after this life. We went back to the table with the rest of the family as though we hadn't had a conversation about life after dying.

After dinner, sitting alone in my car, I berated myself. *You idiot.* I thought. *Why did you tell her?* A powerful voice inside of me responded, "Because that's what happened."

I was now fighting a new kind of struggle. I kept getting spiritual impressions about the people around me. I could sense things that I couldn't see. It wasn't *normal*. Had there been brain damage? Was I going insane?

I also felt like I couldn't tell anyone. I was worried about people judging me or calling me crazy.

Most disturbing of all was that I wanted my life to be over. I found myself imagining ways that I could "accidentally" end my life. I didn't dare make plans to commit suicide. Any time my thoughts strayed in that direction, I could feel that the energy of those thoughts was the exact opposite of what I wanted to return to. While that kept me from harming myself, I no longer felt at home in my own skin, and I longed to return home to live in the real world, not this counterfeit of it. More terrifying was the fear of what if it didn't exist? What if I imagined it and this was all there was? That would be a form of hell.

I decided that I needed professional help. I made an appointment to talk to a psychologist. When we met, I opened up and shared my entire experience with him. He replied that it was probably just my brain filling in the gaps due to lack of oxygen. He told me that it was beyond his ability to help me and referred me to a psychiatrist. When I spoke with the psychiatrist, I shared my experience with him, too.

"Well, Vinney," he said. "It appears that you are suffering from delusions. All of this is happening in your mind."

Something inside of me resisted his conclusion. He was wrong, and I knew it. I finally surrendered to the spiritual impressions that pressed in on me. "Then why do I know these things? Why do I know that—"

I proceeded to share information about him that poured into my brain as fast as I could say it—things that I should not have known about. Personal things that only he knew about his life, and thoughts that he kept inside.

Whatever I said triggered the psychiatrist. He suddenly turned red, stood, and pointed at the door. "Get the ---- out of my office. I never want to see you again."

Stunned, I stopped talking, gathered my things, and moved for the door.

As I walked out, he said, "Something happened to you. There's no way anyone could know those things." He practically slammed the door behind me.

His receptionist was mortified. "I'm so sorry. I've never seen him act like that before. What did you say?"

"I don't know," I said. I left the office.

I felt that the worst thing that had ever happened in my life was being brought back to life.

Chapter 17

HOMESICK

I felt lost.

Maybe it was homesickness for heaven, but I was filled with an overwhelming sense of sadness and loss. I talked to God but felt cut off from Him. Religion had been a big part of my life before this experience, but now I understood how incomplete religious teachings were. I remembered from my time with Drake that religions are usually well intentioned and even help us prepare and progress in this life, but they can only describe a portion of the rainbow's full spectrum. I had seen the true rainbow.

God was so tangible on the other side. I didn't have to see Him to know that He was there. I could feel Him in everything. The grass. The trees. The flowers. Even the water manifested His presence. Yet, here in this life, I had to work to feel His presence. I could feel my separation from God, and it was almost unbearable. All I had here was my family and career. I desperately wanted to go back to my real home, but Drake had told me that I had to return to earth, and that it would be worth it.

So, I prayed. I prayed a lot. As I prayed, I realized that I wasn't alone. I used to think that there was a high and holy man in the clouds waiting to answer my prayers. Now, I could sense that His representatives were right there with me to listen, and to help guide my prayers so that I would say and ask for the right things, if I was open to their guidance. These beings were facilitators as well as guides, helping me to learn to direct my intentions and develop my individual power of creation. I had never sensed that before.

I still felt painfully disconnected from God in this dimension, even though I was striving to connect with Him. I didn't feel Him like I did in the real world, so I assumed that He wasn't in the grass, the trees, or the flowers here. Still, I reached out to Him.

Then, one morning as I looked in the mirror, I saw God in my eyes. That's when everything started to change for me. I realized that in this world, we must find God inside ourselves, and then we can find Him in everything else. After I saw God in my own eyes, I could see Him in the eyes of others, and in the existence of all things. On the other side, you can see the presence of God as an outward manifestation. On this side, you have to connect with God within yourself, and then you can connect with the divine in everyone and everything else.

I now understood that there is a connection to God in *every* single human being. I knew that there is a presence of God in every plant, every animal, every living thing. I understood that there is even God in those things we consider non-living. There is God in everything.

It took months, but I eventually accepted that I was stuck in this realm until it was my time to return, and I decided to change the way I lived my life. I stopped living just for myself and started living with the hope to help and love and lift others. I knew that the way to rise out of my loneliness and despair was through love. As I worked to help lift others up, serving them with love, I could feel the love of God in return.

I discovered that when I raised my frequency through service, I felt God's love more strongly. In that higher state of being, I discovered that I could still communicate with Drake. He taught me that I could communicate with other guides who were there to help me and other people I encountered. When I followed the direction of my guides in serving others, it strengthened my connection with the love of God, and with that love, I knew I could survive.

There was one other thing I needed to do, too. I needed to reconnect with family, and with good friends. And that's what led me to my angel.

Chapter 18

ANOTHER ANGEL

As I made changes in my attitude and actions, I thought about all the good people who had been in my life. One of them was a young woman who I had grown up with. Leslee had called me a few weeks before I died and asked me if I wanted to spend a day with her and her friends. I had turned down her invitation because I thought I had "better things to do." The truth was that Leslee had made religion a central part of her life, while I had been filling my time with work and friends. I had been drifting away from my church.

After I died and returned to this world, I realized that the friends and family that I had been turning away from were far more important in my life than any of the other social circles that I had been running with. A few months after my recovery, I was deleting old contacts on my phone when I saw Leslee's name and had the impression, "You need to call her back."

I called her on a Tuesday.

"Hello?" her voice came through the phone.

"Hi, Leslee. This is Vinney."

"Vinney!" she said enthusiastically. "How have you been?"

"I've been pretty good. How about you?"

"Great. What's up?"

"So, remember a few weeks ago when you invited me to hang out, but I said I couldn't?"

"Yes."

"Well, I was wondering if I could cash in a rain check and get together and do something."

"Sure. Some friends and I are going bowling tonight. Do you want to come?"

"Absolutely."

"Great. If you want, you can come over to my house about seven o'clock and hang out. A bunch of us will be there already."

"Thank you."

"You're welcome. I look forward to seeing you again."

I had plenty of time to get ready, and then made my way there. Leslee didn't live far away, just down the street, actually. I parked my car on the street and walked up to the door. I could hear men's voices inside, talking and laughing.

I knocked, but there was no answer. Not even a break in the conversation. I waited for a minute, then knocked harder. Still no answer.

Determined to not let another chance to reconnect with friends pass me by, I gave the door a solid knuckle pound. I heard a girl yell from somewhere in the house, "Is anyone going to answer that?" I didn't recognize her voice.

No one answered her, either. Then I heard footsteps rush down the stairs to the door, and it opened. The young woman who stood there was blonde, pretty, maybe twenty years old. And she was glowing.

When I say she was glowing, I could see, with my physical eyes, the same light that I had experienced on the other side radiating from her.

I was speechless. So was she. We just stared at each other for what felt like minutes.

Finally, I asked, "Can I come in?"

"Yes, of course. We were just going to play pool upstairs. Do you want to play?"

"Sure. I'd like that."

I followed her up the stairs. When we reached the pool room, there was no one else there. We played, just the two of us. And we talked.

She told me that her name was Andrea. She wasn't the kind of girl that I would have necessarily been attracted to or dated in the past. I had always dated girls with darker hair, and even darker personas. I could see that Andrea was different than any other girl I had ever known. She had a goodness about her that shone. Literally. I could *see* it.

We talked and laughed a lot. Before I knew it, the sun was going down, and we were on our way to the bowling alley.

Andrea climbed into the passenger seat of Leslee's car. The men I had heard talking were Leslee's brother and five of his friends; they all piled into a van together. I drove my car. I wanted to be alone to think about what I was feeling. I didn't understand what was happening. I could feel my being vibrate whenever I was close to her, as if our spirits resonated with each other. It both frightened and fascinated me.

Five more people met us at the bowling alley: three more of Leslee's brother's friends, and my brother and his roommate. The bowling alley was crowded, so, to my disappointment, Andrea was playing in a lane far from mine. I realized that I no longer saw her radiant glow with my physical eyes, but I could feel it every time I looked at her. It was not my usual style to keep track of a girl, but with Andrea, I couldn't resist. I don't know how else to describe it other than that she had a spiritually sweet attraction unlike anyone I had ever met. I recognized that she had a pure and precious innocence that came from God.

I noticed that all of her friends called her Ange.

"Why does everyone call her Ange?" I asked. "I thought her name was Andrea."

"It is. She's such an angel all the time that we just started calling her Angel—Ange for short."

Andrea's game finished first, and she wandered over to the arcade room. I caught up to her as soon as my game ended and said, "It was great meeting you tonight. Can I call you sometime?"

She demurred. "Why don't you give me your number, and maybe I'll call you."

It was the best I was going to get, so I gave her my phone number. It was late, and I had to get up early for work. My parents' house was close by, and they had a spare room I could use, so I decided to sleep there instead of driving all the way home.

As I drove, I reflected on the very real light I saw emanating from her. I knew that Andrea was different, and that she was very special. And despite my persistent thoughts that I still wanted to go back to the other world, I wondered if she might be the light that pulled me out of the darkness I was lost in.

I called Leslee the next morning to see if she wanted to get together again that afternoon. She did, and she brought Andrea with her. Leslee didn't stay long; she said that she had to run an errand but would return in half an hour. She was gone for more than three hours, which gave Andrea and me a chance to get to know each other better.

Andrea seemed to be open to talking about anything, and our conversations ranged from falling stars to quantum physics, the mysteries of life, and a myriad of other subjects. Most important, I felt different around her. She sparked a new energy within me.

A few days later, Andrea and I had lunch together. The waitress who delivered our drinks and appetizers said, "I just love seeing happy married couples. How long have you two been married?"

We were both surprised. I replied, "We actually just met."

"Really? I could have sworn that you two were married."

It was a question we got used to hearing.

Andrea called me Saturday morning.

"Hey, I was wondering if you wanted to come with me and my family to feed ducks at Utah Lake."

I struggled to contain my excitement. "What time?"

"My sister and I will pick you up in an hour."

Andrea and her younger sister, Chelsie, picked me up, and we drove to where the Provo River empties into Utah Lake. Her dad, her fifteen-year-old sister Kim, and her twelve-year-old brother Jacob, met us there.

I didn't interact with her dad much on that day, as he was distracted with the two younger siblings. Chelsie, however, stayed close by and seemed very curious about me. I didn't know it then, but after Andrea arrived home Wednesday night, she woke Chelsie up and spent two hours recounting our evening together.

As the three of us stood on the shore throwing food to the noisy ducks, a woman walked by. She said, "You two are such a beautiful couple. How long have you been married?"

Andrea and I just looked at each other. Chelsie broke the awkward silence with a laugh and said, "Oh, no. They're just friends."

We all laughed along with her, but the lady looked confused. She shook her head as if she was trying to figure out what prompted her to even ask the question.

Andrea and I saw each other almost every day. My mother was happy that we were seeing so much of each other, but Andrea's family was far less excited. Her parents had asked around and learned that I had a bit of a reputation as a bad boy who had "lived a wild life" and cycled through girlfriends. They were understandably worried.

Andrea, of course, had heard the same stories. Even though she acknowledged the positive energy that she felt when we were together, she also had concerns that I was simply looking for another conquest. Still, we continued to grow closer.

I felt deep within me that God had brought us together, and that there was something special in our connection. The same day we fed the ducks at Utah Lake, I was doing my nightly check-in with God, and asked, "Am I supposed to marry Andrea?"

I felt a resounding "*Yes.* You're finally seeing it," from what felt like a chorus of my guides and reinforced by my own intuition.

Still doubting myself, I asked again, and received an even more powerful response. I asked a third time, and I felt a wave of peace wash over me. I was still worried because I didn't know how any of this would work out, or how it was supposed to happen, but I felt relieved at the same time. The answer explained the resonance between us and the strength of our blossoming relationship. That night, I lay down in bed and went straight to sleep.

The next morning, Andrea and I attended a family gathering at my parents' cabin in the south fork of Provo Canyon. It would be the first time she met my parents. We were both unusually silent on the drive as the answer I had received the night before weighed heavily on my mind. I desperately wanted to discuss it with her but was afraid of what might happen.

I felt a strong impression that Andrea had asked the same question last night and had received the same answer. They told me that I had to have the courage to bring it up before the energy between us could return to normal.

I asked, "Did you happen to pray about something important last night?"

Andrea turned to look at me. I could hear the apprehension in her voice. "Yes. Did you?"

I asked my guides, *How do I tell her that we're supposed to get married?*

"Just do it," the answer came.

"I prayed about something pretty important," I said. "I asked three times just to be sure."

"What did you pray about?" she asked.

I took a deep breath, then said, "I prayed to know if we're supposed to get married."

Her eyes opened wide. "What was your answer?"

"That we're supposed to get married."

"It's like you're reading my mind," she said. "I prayed three times last night, too, and asked if I'm supposed to marry you. I got the same answer." The tension between us evaporated.

We arrived at the cabin. We weren't ready to announce an engagement, but my mom already knew. She told me later that she had known where this was going the first time I told her about Andrea.

Andrea showed me how well someone could connect with spiritual light and be in tune with higher frequencies. I had to die to know what it feels like to feel God's presence, but it came naturally for her.

In addition to helping me through the darkness of re-entry into the mortal world, Andrea opened my heart to a richer, more fulfilling mortal experience. She showed me the world through her eyes, bringing purity and wonder into my life. With her, I realized that I was passing up happiness every day.

Andrea helped me elevate my life in other ways. My standards for language and entertainment were quite low, influenced by my career in construction and the people I worked with. Even after my experience, I still had a lot of growing to do in order to reform my old earthly habits. One day, I asked her if she wanted to go to the theater to watch a newly released movie with me.

"What's in it?" she asked.

"What do you mean?"

"Like how much violence? Are there sex scenes? What about the kind of language they use?"

"I don't know. I just heard it's really good."

She put her hands on her hips. "Vinney, you've been teaching me how to eat better and pay more attention to what I put in my body, right? What if we went to a buffet and I started putting some of everything on my plate?"

"I'd say that you'd feel better if you were more careful about what you ate."

"Isn't it the same with what you put in your mind?"

I could almost feel Drake telling me, "See? That's what we were talking about."

That was just one of the many ways that she inspired and encouraged me to raise my frequency. Her example and influence inspired me to be better.

Above all, Andrea helped me to understand that family is the most important thing in life. I grew to know that my own family was something to cherish, and that the way to share and develop that love was through spending time with them. In my old life, whenever my family had a get-together, I always found something "more important" to do. Family, including my own, was such a priority for Andrea that it became a priority for me. It was this new appreciation of family that led to the event that confirmed to me once and for all that what I'd experienced on the other side had really happened.

Chapter 19

THE POWER OF FAMILY

My FATHER'S FAMILY had a regular summer reunion in a little town called Afton in the rugged Star Valley region of western Wyoming. It's the sort of thing that I would have usually been "too busy" to go to before, and I hadn't been in over a decade, but this year, due to Andrea's influence, I decided to go. It helped that Andrea was able to go with me.

I couldn't remember ever having more fun at a reunion. I took every opportunity to introduce my fiancée to all of my relatives. Throughout the day, everyone kept asking us if we were going to the show that night.

The "show" was a pageant that the local high school produced about the history of Star Valley. My father's ancestors were among the first settlers in the area in the 1880s, so it sounded like an interesting way to spend the evening. The high school drama club had turned the football field into an outdoor theater, with a movie screen and a wooden stage.

The turnout was good for such a small town, especially since this was the second night of the performance. Most of the four hundred or so attendees were clustered in the bottom half of the bleachers. I still felt claustrophobic in crowds, so we found an open spot near the top, directly in front of the movie screen.

Even though it was July, the air turned chilly as soon as the sun disappeared. Throughout the pageant, the local children, teenagers, and adults related the history of Star Valley through singing, dancing, and skits. They alternated between performing on the stage and showing pictures on the screen, showing the area's rich history and my family's part in it.

The show's organizers had gathered historical photographs of the early settlement, and shared letters and journal entries from the era, teaching about the first settlers in the area and the hardships they faced working to carve a town out of the rough wilderness. They shared stories of the people who founded Afton, most of whom were part of the local religious community.

As the night wore on, and the temperature continued to drop, my interest faded, so when Andrea said, "I'm getting really cold." I said, "Let's go."

As I stood to go, Andrea didn't move. She seemed entranced by an image on the movie screen.

"Did you change your mind?" I asked.

She turned to me, her eyes wide. "Vinney, is that your guide?"

I turned back to see a black and white photograph of one of the settlers projected on the screen. I felt as if a pitcher of ice water had been poured down my back. It was Drake.

"That's him, right?" It was yet another example of how Andrea lived in tune with higher frequencies.

I just stood there as tears rolled down my cheeks. It was him; his piercing eyes were unmistakable. The beard he wore as my guide was cleaner on the ends, and a little longer, and his hair was combed back in the picture, not flowing like when I met him. He looked a lot older in the picture than when I knew him in spirit, yet, I knew it was him. Everything matched.

Everything except his name. Below the image of the man was written the name "Chrs. D. Cazier."

"That's him," I finally said.

Andrea asked me to share more about my experience with Drake with her on the drive back to the hotel, but I was too shaken to even speak. Seeing Drake again opened a floodgate of emotions that I was simply not prepared for. A torrent of thoughts and feelings churned inside of me as the two worlds inside my head collided.

I realized that up until that moment I had, to some degree, rationalized my experience on the other side as an illusion. I had even considered that the psychologist's explanation was correct—that what I thought I saw was just my brain filling in the gaps due to lack of oxygen.

I had a big reason for not wanting to believe what I'd experienced. To accept the reality of the other world would mean that I would not only have to change the way I saw the world, but myself and everyone else as well.

It meant that I would have to radically change the way I lived my life and, if there's one thing we humans resist, it's change—which is why we spend much more time and effort confirming what we already believe than seeking truth.

But my brain could not have invented the name and face of a man who had lived over a century ago—a man I didn't, until that night, even know existed. I could no longer hide behind the plausible denial that Drake and what he showed me were just figments of an oxygen-starved brain.

My experience had been real, and I could no longer deny it. Still, one thing puzzled me. I recognized the last name Cazier as my grandmother's maiden name, and "Chrs" was an abbreviation for Charles. But my guide had introduced himself as Drake.

The next day, Andrea and I approached my grandmother.

"Grandma," I asked, "did you know a Charles Cazier?"

"Of course," she said. "That's great-grandpa Drake."

"He went by Drake?"

"That's what everyone called him."

I was once again overcome with emotion. Drake was my great-great-great-grandfather.

Chapter 20

GRANDMA DONA

ANDREA AND I WERE MARRIED a month later. A few months earlier, my company had bid on a project to frame a custom home in Alaska, and two weeks after our wedding, my boss and I were off to Fairbanks, Alaska, to fulfill that one-month contract. After we arrived, the general contractor asked us to frame a second home, too, which stretched the job to two months. We worked over ten hours a day, six days a week.

There was no cell phone reception in our area, so at the end of each day, I would talk to Andrea on a pay phone outside our hotel. Our conversations would last as long as I could stand being outside in the cold Alaska evenings, usually between thirty minutes and an hour. Our conversations brightened the monotony of my long days. Despite the distance, we grew closer.

Being away from Andrea was an enormous struggle. Once again, I felt cut off from unconditional love and separated from joy. I was far away from where I wanted to be, stuck in a remote, cold place working hard every day, and struggling to keep my spirits up. In some ways, it felt like I was coming back from the dead all over again.

As much as I wished for Andrea to be with me, every avenue we explored to have her join me in Alaska led to a dead end. Though it was painful at the time, our time apart taught us how important we were to each other and helped us to make sure the little issues of life didn't get in the way of our relationship.

I was anxious to get back home, and the last three weeks of the project we worked twelve-hour days, seven days a week. I had one week left when Andrea said that my dad wanted to discuss something with me. We arranged a time to talk.

"How's Alaska?" he asked. "I loved the fishing when I was up there. How do you like the fishing?"

"There's no time for fishing," I said. "I've just been working the whole time."

"Oh, that's too bad. Try to do some fishing while you're up there."

I was still wondering why he called. "Is everything okay?"

"We're fine," he said. "But Grandma's struggling. Her health is starting to wane. She's tired of living with your uncle, and she's getting really obstinate about it. She really wants to move back home to Afton, but she'd be all alone up there. Your mom and I are asking around to see if anyone could go and help her live out the last few months of her life. Would you and Andrea be willing to stay with her? I know that's asking a lot, but it would allow her to go back home."

It *was* a lot to ask. Finally, I said, "I'm almost done up here and will be back home soon. I'll talk to Andrea about it."

"I appreciate it. Thanks, son."

"Sure thing. I love you, Dad."

"I love you, too."

I immediately called Andrea and told her about my conversation with my father. We decided to pray for guidance. When we did, we both felt guided to live with my grandmother in Star Valley for however long we were needed there.

I returned to Utah in the middle of October. Andrea and I spent a week packing up our few possessions, then drove four hours north to Afton a few days before Halloween.

Grandma Dona's house was just as I remembered it. The two thousand square foot, two-story brick home had four bedrooms and no basement. It had been built in the 1950s and was where Grandma had lived for almost all of her married life.

We carried our belongings inside and settled in. The house had a cabin feel; the downstairs rooms were covered in wood paneling. The carpet was vintage 1970s brown pile, with light and dark patches. It was heated by an oil burning stove that sat in the same spot as the wood burning stove it had replaced decades before.

My grandmother was in her eighties when we moved in. She had a ready smile, framed by a full head of white hair done up in a short, roller-set style. Her wardrobe consisted almost entirely of seventies era button-up shirts and polyester slacks, with dresses for Sundays. She always wore a housecoat at home and dressed up to go to the grocery store. She had a kind, calm voice, and would say, "Oh, my word," about everything. She had a hard time initiating the words "I love you," but showed her love through her actions; usually by baking. She was famous for her chicken noodle soup and her cookies.

Andrea helped Grandma with tasks that she could no longer do herself. That included cooking, cleaning, dressing, and showering. I quickly found a job in construction, and between traveling to job sites and the actual work, I was often gone more than twelve hours a day. We always had dinner together, though. Grandma called it "supper." Those evenings we had together are treasured memories.

Growing up, I always thought of my grandma as a strict authoritarian figure. She was always after us to do what we were supposed to: take off our shoes in the house, wash our hands, eat everything on our plate, and help Grandpa with his chores. Living with her now, though, I was able to see a different side of her personality. I learned that she had had a life full of aspirations and achievements.

She was an identical twin, and she and her sister, Dora, had been best friends who did everything together throughout their lives. They were born in 1918, three months after their father left to fight in the trenches of Belgium and France in World War I. One evening, she told Andrea and me the story of the day they were born.

"Daddy was in a trench on the front lines, and two faces appeared to him. Six months later he found out that two bouncy, round baby girls were born."

Grandma and Dora grew up on a farm in Star Valley without indoor plumbing, electricity, or telephones. They attended Star Valley High School, where they shared a role in the school performance of *Huckleberry Finn*, taking turns in each act. She laughed about how much fun they had as twins and told us how they often fooled their boyfriends.

Dona and Dora were in a local television commercial, acting as spokeswomen for a local lawnmower company. Grandma also worked as a telephone switchboard operator, but the job made her so nervous that she had to quit.

Other experiences included working in a hardware store, a clothing store, and a gift shop. Her favorite job was at the Star Valley creamery, where she wrapped butter squares, four squares per pound.

We spent nearly every night in conversation. She loved the chance we gave her to share her life stories with someone.

About a month after we moved in, Grandma's twin sister died. Grandma became very depressed after that, and her health declined rapidly. Her back hurt, and she began to lose feeling in her legs. She would sit in her reclining chair most of the day. Andrea helped her bathe and use the toilet and massaged her legs every day. In addition, she would do all of the house cleaning and cooking. It was a struggle to get Grandma to eat, and she required constant coaxing. She would often call for help from Andrea in the middle of the night.

Grandma felt as if she had lost part of herself when her twin sister died and struggled to cope with her death. I considered that relating my own experience with death might help bring her peace.

One night after dinner I said, "You know, Grandma, I died and was brought back."

"I heard about that," she said.

"Do you want to know more about that?"

She waved her hand in the air. "No, it's all phooey." I wanted to tell her more anyway, but Spirit always told me no.

Weeks went by. We spent Thanksgiving together and prepared for Christmas. Andrea stayed busy doing all the things that Grandma would have done if she had been able to. Thanksgiving meant preparing a full spread of turkey, potatoes, sweet potatoes, and everything else in a traditional Thanksgiving dinner, even though the only guests were my mom and my aunt Dawnette.

We spent days cooking treats for the neighbors. I set up the tree, and Andrea decorated it with ornaments Grandma had collected over the decades. Each ornament had its designated spot on the tree and had to be positioned just so.

Grandma was fastidious about cleaning, so when Andrea wasn't cooking or tending to Grandma's needs, she would spend her days cleaning and organizing, directed by Grandma from her chair in the living room. One of her tasks was going through a set of filing cabinets, throwing away old papers that didn't matter anymore.

Grandma had a habit of saving newspaper clippings with stories about people she knew and had collected a lifetime of stories from the Afton, Wyoming, newspaper. In the small farming community, everyone knew everyone else. Any time there was a birth, death, or graduation announcement, she would save it. Rodeos were central to farm and country life in Afton, and Grandpa had been a champion cutter racer, where a pair of horses pull a small chariot around a track. She would also save news about champions from the annual state fair, rodeo wins, and other items of interest in farm country life.

A few days before Christmas, as Andrea was clearing out another drawer, she discovered an old maroon, faux-leather binder full of folders and document sleeves. As she thumbed through the old pages, one of the documents caught her eye. It was the transcript of a blessing that was given to one of the original settlers in the valley—Charles Drake Cazier. He had been called by church leaders to oversee the leadership of several congregations in the valley. Drake did not feel qualified or capable enough for so much responsibility and had sought counsel from another local leader who was called a "patriarch"—someone tasked with giving inspired blessings to people in that same area.

Andrea showed me the paper as soon as I got home. The blessing said that Drake was going to be a guide, or escort, for those of his blood, as well as others who needed his love and assistance in transition from this life to the next.

Here was another remarkable confirmation about my guide, Drake. What a wonderful guide he had been. I never felt one inkling of judgment, not a single malicious thought, not one negative feeling. I would have felt it if there was. All he ever expressed, all I ever felt from him, was pure, unconditional, and unequivocal love.

I was excited to share the blessing and my experience with my grandmother. I waited for a day when she was in good spirits. Christmas Day was a happy day for everyone, full of visiting friends and family. That evening, after the excitement had settled down and our visitors were busy in other parts of the house, Andrea and I sat down with my grandmother. I showed her Drake's blessing and explained that he had been my guide. I told her about all the wondrous things he had taught me.

When I finished, Grandma just sat silently as she stared off into the distance. Then she opened up and told us that she had been concerned about one of her family members. She loved that person dearly, but they had had a hard life and made some decisions that made it appear that they were destined for what we traditionally consider hell. She was deeply and bitterly worried about the future of this person that she loved so deeply.

"Grandma," I explained, "this grand human experiment *is* hell. But it isn't our final destination. Life here is only a training ground. On the other side, the worst of us become better, and the best of us become greater. We all grow and progress as much and as fast as we are able."

We sat together in silence as she reflected on what I had shared with her. I still had a question burning inside of me, and after waiting several minutes, I asked, "Is there anything you can tell me about Drake? Anything at all?"

Grandma looked deep into her early memories. "I met him when I was a little girl. Very little. But I still remember that whenever he held me, he would look into my eyes. I always felt that those blue eyes could just see inside my soul."

I knew exactly what she meant. I had experienced it, too, just like that.

It was a third confirmation that my time in the world beyond ours was real. The first was seeing the photo of Drake. The second was the blessing he had been given. And now here, my grandmother, who had known him in this life, described him just as I had experienced him in the next one.

It took my grandmother a while to process what I explained to her about judgment and the next life, that God will not give up on any of us, ever, but eventually she was able to embrace the idea that God had a special path for her family member, and they were going to be fine no matter what. Once she accepted that truth, we saw a change in her, both emotionally and physically. Over time, her back stopped hurting her, and feeling started to return to her legs.

Chapter 21

MY LIFE AFTER DEATH

GRANDMA DONA TRANSITIONED to the next world the following February—a little more than a year after I had come back from there. Her death marked the beginning of a new chapter for Andrea and me as we left Afton to create a life for ourselves.

Of course, I still had a lot of growth ahead of me, with plenty of hard things to go through and a lot to learn, but I live my life differently than I did before. I continue to do my best to be aware of the needs of others and to help those who I can. As I strive to be open to spiritual impressions, I have become hyperaware of what is going on around me.

Different people perceive spiritual impressions in different ways. For me, they feel like an energy wave carrying information. As I sift through that information, I can recognize someone's need and receive guidance from the other side on how to do my part to fulfill it. Sometimes, it is a physical need.

Sometimes, I pass along what feels like a random piece of advice to someone, even if it makes no sense to me.

One hot summer day, a friend and I were driving to a local café to have lunch. I saw a homeless man walking down the street. I sensed that he was tired and hungry and saw that in a few minutes, he would pass by the café we were going to.

I sent my thoughts to the man's guides and asked, "Is he going to the same café we are?"

I felt the reply, "No, he's going to keep walking past it."

"Can you urge him to go inside? It's a hot day, and he can cool off for a minute."

"Yes."

My friend and I entered the café and ordered our food. I ordered an extra lunch.

"You must be really hungry," said my friend.

I smiled at him. "You'll see."

When our food was ready, I set my meal on the table, then took the tray with the extra food to the drink machine. I filled up my drink, then a drink for the homeless man.

As I finished filling the second drink, the homeless man walked in through the front door and sat down at a table. I walked over to him, set the tray down in front of him, and said, "Here's your lunch." I met his puzzled look with a smile and returned to my table, where my friend sat in wide-eyed surprise at what had just happened.

As amazing as that experience might seem, I was simply made aware of a need and acted to meet that need. I've learned that the more we are mindful of the needs of those around us, the happier we are, and the fewer needs we feel for ourselves.

We are designed by our Creator to find joy in helping others. Whether it's us doing the helping, or being the one receiving it, we are vitalized by experiencing God's creations serving each other. It can't be otherwise.

Personally, I am still working to master the principles that Drake taught me. Every day, I strive to live outside of my own needs and help at least a few people every day. Most days I am successful, but not always. It's a process.

I have also learned to live life with passion and to love with passion. Where you find true passion, you will find souls that are fulfilling their mission in life. Divine passion is what drives us to learn and to grow and to build. Divine passion is what fosters creation in relationships, in careers, in ourselves. Divine passion is what creates love. When someone has that kind of fire within themselves, their life lights up like a bonfire on a dark night. When they add the love of God, that bonfire radiates a warmth that comforts others in the cold nights of life.

God's passion built the universe. It was His passionate love for us that built the cosmos. It's passion that creates. It's His passionate love that knows each and every single one of us. It's His passionate love that knows you personally, individually. He knows your every thought. He knows everything you've ever wanted, desired, or done.

You don't have to fear that He knows. God is a father of absolute love. He knows why you make mistakes. He knows before you even make them. But He also knows your potential. He knows what you can become, and He longs for you to develop that potential, to grow into it and become all that you can be.

I challenge you to take the opportunity to grow your soul every day—to let no day be wasted.

I implore you to watch out for harmful influences to your body and spirit. Avoid taking in things that will dull your sensitivity to spiritual things, whether they are physical, mental, emotional, or spiritual. Guard against shows, movies, and other media and activities that will pull your spirit down. Unplug from technology that distracts and controls you, whether it is a phone, computer, or any other technology that controls your life. If you're not careful and intentional about it, technology can turn you into a robot wandering through life without the spiritual influence He intended.

Seek good. Fill your life with good food, good media, and good friends. Enrich your life and enlarge your soul.

If you are skeptical about there being a spiritual side to our existence—even if you don't believe it at all—I challenge you to test it. Start by keeping gratitude in your heart, and seek for answers to your questions. It may take time to learn how guidance and answers come to you but keep trying. Strive to develop a greater awareness of impressions, of the thoughts that come to you, and of good ideas that can improve your life. As you practice and strive to reach out, I promise you that His universe will answer.

As you reach outward and upward, you will discover truths in your own life. You will find loving direction coming directly from God. You will also find that you are already part of a spiritual community—a grand family of enlightened beings. As you connect to God's light, you will begin to recognize that light all around you. You will begin to wonder how you hadn't seen it. You will actually feel and recognize the presence of God, the presence that I saw and felt, that I smelled and tasted in the grass and the trees and the flowers in heaven.

I have seen that light coming from my brothers and sisters of all colors, all cultures, all races, all lifestyles, all religions. It's when I find someone else from my spirit tribe, God's tribe, that I experience my happiest moments. It is that love that changed me forever, and it can change you, too.

I am a father now. Andrea and I have taught these principles to our daughter since she was a child. Now, she is entering her teenage years, and the light is familiar to her. She will sometimes mention to us when she notices its presence or absence in others. She tells us when she goes to a friend's house, and there isn't the same love energy that she feels at home. I keep reminding her that whatever she watches, reads, or listens to, she makes it a part of herself. In all things, we are careful to lead her in love. Love will persuade far more than using authority or anger. She is evidence of how living these principles can help us to know the light. She understands the light, and she dwells in the light.

My hope is that sharing what I learned on the "other side" will help to build the light in you, and in others it may touch, to spread God's light throughout the world, across all cultures, across all religions, to anyone who is ready for this message of love and light.

There is more to my story. I was allowed to see some amazing things that are going to happen in the future. These are not scary things. They are glorious things. There is reason for hope.

Most important, know that God loves you. He knows you

personally, and He loves you personally. He knows every loving, beautiful thought you've ever had. He also knows every dark thought and action. His light and love are enough to wash it away. Darkness cannot exist in His light. Let the judgment go, of yourself as well as others.

God loves all of his creations and is constantly reaching out to us. All of us. The word "all" is difficult for our finite minds to comprehend, but it's true. You are part of His all. That deserves repeating. *You are part of His all.* He loves you, as you are, knowing your potential as only He can.

God is love. It's up to us to embrace it.

READY FOR MORE?

Now that you've learned the ten principles that Drake taught Vincent, you are ready for *Living the Light*, an activity guide to help you live the ten principles and increase light and love in your life.

Learn how to get your copy of *Living the Light* at **TheLightAfterDeath.com**

You can also visit that site for additional content:

- Andrea Tolman's perspective on meeting Vincent
- Photos of Vincent, Drake, and Grandma Dona
- Additional examples of how Vincent and Andrea's daughter listens to spiritual guidance

We also invite you to join *Living God's Light*, a global community created to increase the light in your life and help spread God's Light in the world.

LivingGodsLight.com

ACKNOWLEDGMENTS

CREATING A BOOK IS A TEAM EFFORT. The authors are deeply grateful for the countless people who have provided support and encouragement throughout this process. We would like to thank a few of those contributors in particular:

Richard Paul Evans, our mentor, dear friend, and brother in God's Light.

Diane Glad, for freely sharing her many gifts, especially the precious gifts of enthusiasm and optimism.

Alan Smith, for transcribing the audio of Vinney's experience, and for his consistent advice, encouragement, and perspective that moved this project forward.

Sydny Miner, editor extraordinaire, whose insights and questions brought hazy details into sharp focus and elevated the entire book.

Lola Taylor, our Web wizard with the creativity of Edison and the patience of Job.

Drake, Vinney's guide on this side and the other, and Lynn's guide in crafting the book.

In addition, Vinney would like to acknowledge:

My amazing best friend and wife Andrea Tolman, and my two incredible kids, Emma Grace & William Kurtis.

Lynn, the string to my kite. Thank you for keeping me on task and asking all the right questions.

My real Angels: June, Barbara, Della, Maya, Clete, Michael, Paul, and Geronimo.

S.F.H. my soul brother, thank you for teaching me there are others just like me in the world.

Bishop Jeffries, thank you for exemplifying the stewardship and love of God for His children.

And Lynn would like to acknowledge:

Donna Taylor. My perfect match literally made in heaven. Here's to eternity.

Devon, Sydney, Joshua, Kai, Margaret, and Ari. (And to those yet to join us, include yourself here, too.)

Devon & Deanne Taylor. It's a special thing when your parents are also among your best friends.

Brenda, Paula, Gary, Diana, Alan, Lola, and Scott. Siblings in body and in spirit. I love you all.

Andy, Chris, Craig, Matthew, Ricky, and Vinney. Kajir brothers forever.

Lola, Lisle, Lynn, and Nita. Thank you for continuing to lead and guide me.

And to the rest of my guides. I may not know your names yet, but I recognize your presence now. Thank you.

About the Authors

VINCENT TODD TOLMAN was born in Arlington, Texas, and has since traveled around the world, living in both Cambodia and Thailand. He has worked as a home builder, computer technician, and producer for the television and film industry. He loves animals, meditating, and spending time in nature. His greatest priorities are his relationship with his Creator, his family, and the people he meets. He currently lives in Las Vegas, Nevada with his wife, Andrea, and their two children.

LYNN D. TAYLOR graduated from Embry-Riddle Aeronautical University with a degree in Aerospace Engineering prior to serving in the U.S. Air Force as a fighter pilot. In addition to writing, Lynn works in county government leadership and is a board member of The Christmas Box International. He lives in northern Utah with his wife (and calculus tutor), Donna, and their four sons.